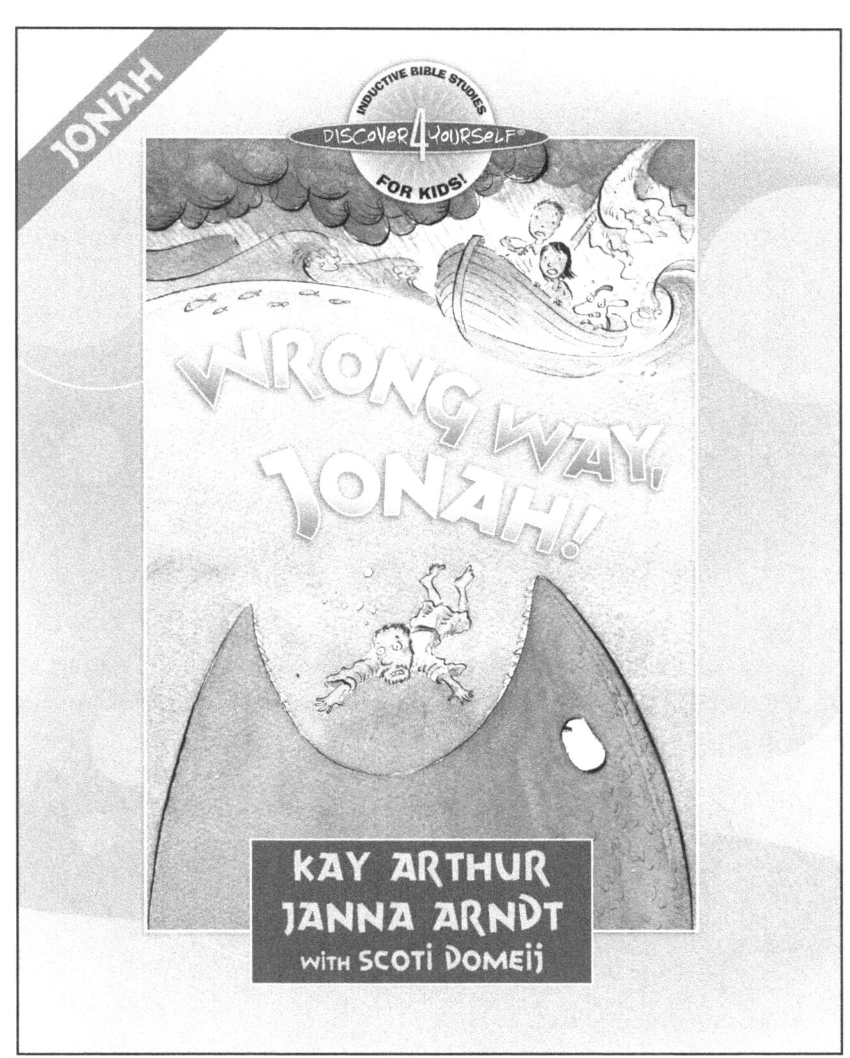

TEACHER GUIDE

Elizabeth A. McAllister, Ed. D.

WRONG WAY, JONAH! TEACHER GUIDE
Published by Precept Ministries of Reach Out, Inc.
P. O. Box 182218
Chattanooga, TN 37422

ISBN 978-1-888655-37-7

D4Y Teacher Guides were made possible by the generous gift of a long-time friend of Precept Ministries.

Author Photo and Cover by John Phillips

Graphics Design by Michele Walker

WRONG WAY, JONAH!
TEACHER GUIDE
TABLE OF CONTENTS

WRONG WAY, JONAH!
TEACHER GUIDE

Introduction

Thank you for selecting this Bible study for your child and/or class. Leading children to read, observe, interpret, and apply the Bible for themselves offers them a bridge from hearsay to real truth. As they learn to be comfortable with the idea that they can read the Bible, they will take the task seriously.

The Discover 4 Yourself series is designed to lead young students through the process of inductive study: question, question, question, search, think, understand, and apply. They will be comfortable with this process only after you prove that the possibility is within their reach.

WRONG WAY, JONAH! is a study of the book of Jonah—a factual story with a moral. Students will learn a lot about God's grace—how it works and how it perseveres. Jonah was rebellious and God had to work hard to get him to do what He commanded him. It was a frightening experience being in the belly of a great fish for three days but Jonah learned this hard way how much God cares for a wicked and far-away people he didn't think God cared for. God gave Jonah a fresh start to wipe the slate clean—to repent and do what He originally commanded him to do. A whole city repented at His preaching, and the Lord blessed it. It's a wonderful lesson for all of us.

In preparation for leading ***WRONG WAY, JONAH!*** please work through each "Day" on your own before consulting the Teacher Guide. Since this is an Inductive Bible Study, your teaching will be more effective if you do the work first and God reveals His truth to you.

Whether you're homeschooling a child, teaching a Sunday school class, teaching in a Christian school, or simply using these studies for your child's quiet time or family Bible study, this Teacher Guide will show you how to clearly and carefully lead each child through Inductive Bible study. We offer suggestions to guide you step-by-step. *Instructional Strategies* explains why certain activities are used throughout the book. Choose the activities that best fit your situation.

Homeschooling Parents and Family Bible Study

We suggest you do one "Day" per day unless it's too much for your child's reading and/or writing skills. You can work with your child and discuss what you learn together or let him/her work independently, saving discussion times for later.

You may want to join or create a homeschool group that meets once a week to do these studies. The teacher will assign a week of homework in class. The following week the teacher will lead the students to discuss what they discovered, how to apply it, and to work on any creative elements included in the study or play a game to review what they have learned.

Sunday School Teachers

To use these studies in a weekly Sunday school class we suggest you do one "Day" together with your children each week in class, since you will have children from different backgrounds, even some from families that are not members of or even regularly attend a church.

Each Sunday briefly review the prior Sunday's work to put them in context for the next day of study in their book. After completing a week in the book you may want to have a "Game Time Sunday" to review the material before you move on to the next week. Game time makes learning fun for children and shows you the extent to which they understand what they learned.

You can keep the books at church and have the children take home verses on index cards or pieces of paper to memorize.

Classroom Teachers

Generally, classroom teachers face many different learning abilities within their groups. It is important for you to understand these different learning abilities so that you can meet each child where he or she is so that no one is left behind during the process.

It is important for you to bring in *schemata* (background information) for students to draw on. If you tie studies to something children already know, they will grasp the lessons clearly.

Grasp is also affected by *metacognition*—the ability to monitor understanding of the text. Students must be able to perform several functions to develop metacognitive control over reading and understanding. He or she must be able to:

1. Ask first, "What do I already know about this topic?" then, "Do I have enough information to understand this text?" Answers to these questions will directly influence the use of the inductive method.

2. Identify the purpose for reading each selection.

3. Focus on particular information.

4. Monitor understanding by recalling background knowledge and relating it to the context by asking questions like: "How am I doing?" "Am I keeping the big picture in mind?" "Am I bogged down?" "If so, how do I fix it—reread the passages or ask for help?" (Nothing wrong with the latter.)

5. Evaluate understanding of the context by asking, "What did I learn?" With respect to Inductive Bible Study, "How do I apply this information?"

Instructional Strategies

Writing as a response reinforces learning and so this method is prevalent in these books. Encourage students to share ideas and insights with you and other students.

Reading is the highest intellectual activity of the human experience. More sectors of the brain are active than in other endeavors including mathematics and flying an airplane. It's the most totally interactive processing of information, even when children are reading Mother Goose.

Take time for students to read aloud with a friend. Reading *out loud* and listening promote interactions between the brain's left and right hemispheres and activate little-used pathways. Reading *silently* activates a much smaller part of the brain.

Give students a chance to express themselves at every opportunity. This forces them to retrieve information stored in their *schemata* (background knowledge) for application to new information. What better opportunity is there than to *inductively* look at curriculum and context?

You will notice that you are asked to read some content aloud as students follow along. This frees unsure readers to focus on context rather than decoding strategies. By doing this, you will remove stumbling blocks to understanding; otherwise, reluctant readers will be convinced that inductive study is impossible for them—the last thought you want to instill!

We have included weekly quizzes with memory verses and also multiple-choice questions that will force students to think about what they have learned. Based on how they answer these questions, you will know whether they have grasped the material adequately.

In view of this sparse introduction to learning requirements for success, it's important that you apply strategies that lead students to develop the ability to self-monitor understanding of context each step of the way. These **Teacher Guides** offer suggestions to assure that students, regardless of their abilities, will learn to read the Bible with understanding as you lead them, step-by-step, through the Inductive Study Method.

Discover 4 Yourself Objectives

The Discover 4 Yourself series objectives are not the same as the behavioral objectives of general subject matter. The books contain outstanding biblical subjects of course, but they are written *primarily* to be a tool for young students to learn the Inductive Bible Study Method.

Playing an instrument well requires repetition and application of skills learned. Similarly, effective study is developed by repeated practice and good role modeling of an outstanding study method. Accordingly these **Teacher Guides** contain global objectives for the student *and the teacher*.

We'll start with the teacher.

Discover 4 Yourself Teacher Guide Objectives

✓ To help the teacher identify students' metacognitive needs as they read texts.

✓ To show the teacher how to model use of the Inductive Study Method so students will be able to apply the techniques independently when studying God's Word.

✓ To offer the teacher effective teaching strategies to assure that students succeed when they study the Bible.

Discover 4 Yourself Student Workbook Objectives

✓ To learn how to read, observe, and interpret the Bible for themselves.

✓ To practice this method independently within an encouraging environment.

All Scripture quotations are taken from the New American Standard Bible®, © 1960, 1962, 1963, 1968, 1971, 1972, 1973, 1975, 1977, 1995 by The Lockman Foundation. Used by permission. (www.Lockman.org)

DISCOVER 4 YOURSELF is a registered trademark of The Hawkins Children's LLC. Harvest House Publishers, Inc., is the exclusive licensee of the federally registered trademark DISCOVER 4 YOURSELF.

Illustrations © 2009 by Steve Bjorkman

Cover by Left Coast Design, Portland, Oregon

WRONG WAY, JONAH!
Copyright © 1999/2010 by Precept Ministries International
Published by Harvest House Publishers
Eugene, Oregon 97402
www.harvesthousepublishers.com

ISBN 978-0-7369-2819-9

Printed in the United States of America

10   11   12   13   14   15   16   17   / ML-NI /   10   9   8   7   6   5   4   3   2   1

1 (page 3)

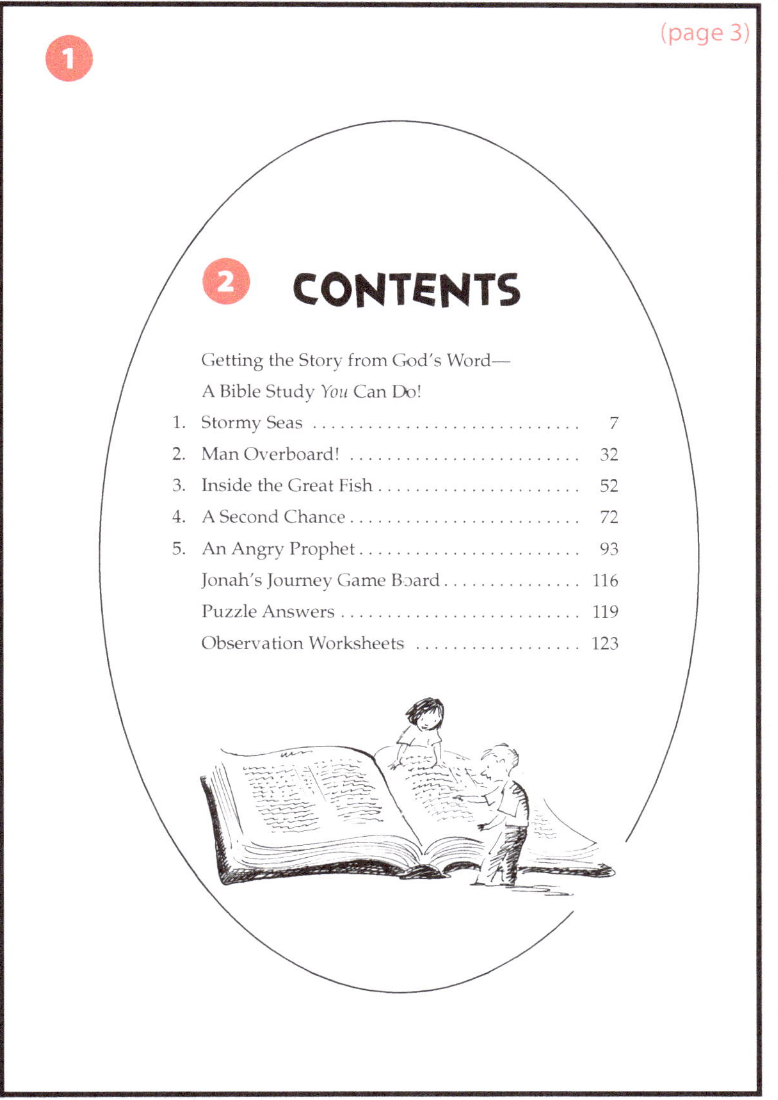

CONTENTS

Getting the Story from God's Word—
A Bible Study *You* Can Do!

Guided Instruction

1 Give each student a copy of ***Wrong Way, Jonah***!

2 Turn to the CONTENTS page and lead students through a quick overview of the book. Point out the structure of each chapter, noting that there will be a lesson and activities to do each day for five days.

"Stormy Seas" (Jonah 1:1–9) 7

A prophet named Jonah thought he could get away from God. He ran when God told him to go to Nineveh to carry His message to the people. But Jonah did not want to go there. Do you think you can run away from God's commands? Jonah found out that God is everywhere and would find him and do something. There are consequences to disobeying God.

"Man Overboard!" (Jonah 1:10–17) 32

God showed Jonah He means business when He gives an order. Because Jonah disobeyed, God disciplined him. He sent a great storm, endangering the lives of everyone on board. The frightened sailors threw Jonah overboard when he recommended this. God then sent a great fish to swallow Jonah. What a messy situation!

"Inside the Great Fish" (Jonah 2) 52

Jonah remained in "the great fish" for three days and three nights. Imagine what that would be like. Smelly? Dark? Stuffy? But Jonah prayed to God. After Jonah confessed his disobedience, God caused the fish to vomit him up on dry land. Whew!

"A Second Chance" (Jonah 3) 72

Even though Jonah defied God, God was merciful and gracious. He gave Jonah a new opportunity to preach judgment coming to Nineveh within forty days. Do you think the people will believe God's message? Will God judge or save Nineveh? How will Jonah respond either way?

"An Angry Prophet" (Jonah 4) 93

Of all people to become angry after God gave him a second chance! When the people repented at his message of coming judgment, Jonah was very angry, so angry he asked God to take His life so he wouldn't have to watch God's grace and mercy poured out on the people of Nineveh. How selfish! And so Jonah suffered more because of this attitude of unforgiveness. Do you think God wants us to hold back His message of reconciliation?

3 Turn back to page 7 and begin the study of "Stormy Seas."

Guided Instruction

(page 5)

Hey, guys, come on up to the tree house! There is a big news story unfolding in Israel that we want you to help us uncover. Molly, Sam (the great face-licking detective beagle), and I are planning our new Bible adventure. By the way, my name is Max. We want you to join us as we create our own newspaper—the *Nineveh News*—to get the scoop on a prophet named Jonah, plus one of Israel's old enemies, the nation of Assyria.

This is an amazing news story that the world needs to know about! WHAT do we need to investigate? WHO is Jonah? WHAT does God tell him to do? WHERE does Jonah go? WHAT happens then? WHAT is God's plan for Jonah and the people in Nineveh? And HOW does Jonah feel about God's plan?

You'll get the answers to all these questions and scoop the competition as you head out on the scene by going straight to God's Word, the Bible the source of all truth, and by asking God's Spirit to lead and guide you.

(page 6)

You also have this book, which is an inductive Bible study. The word *inductive* means you go straight to the Bible *yourself* to investigate what the book of Jonah shows you about an awesome God and a man named Jonah. In inductive Bible study you discover for yourself what the Bible says and means.

Aren't you excited? Grab your Bible and get ready for an unbelievable adventure as you uncover the *real* story about a man who tried to run away from God. Then you can spread the news to show other people WHO God is, HOW much He loves us, and WHY we should obey Him the *first* time!

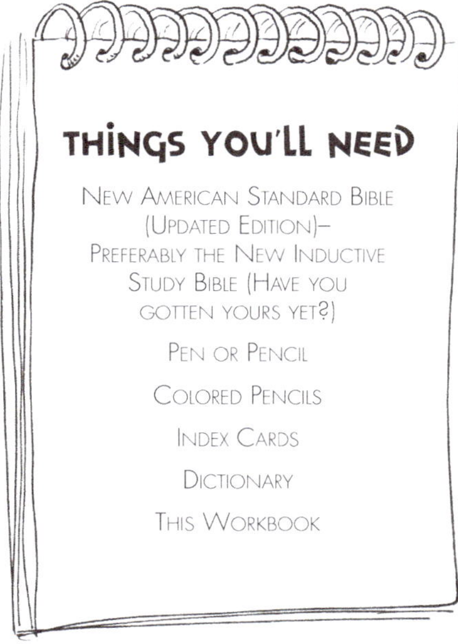

Guided Instruction

WEEK 1

You are about to read a factual story of God's grace and mercy toward a rebellious people. Ask the Lord to help you understand His Word today.

 Read Jonah 1:1–9 and "Our Assignment" beginning on page 7.

1

JONAH 1:1-9

"We're glad you're here!" Max called out. "Are you ready to uncover a very important news story so the world can learn about God and His prophet named Jonah?" Max paused for a breath.

"This is going to be so cool. Newspapers help people find out what is going on in the world. Mr. Davis, the publisher of our daily newspaper, is going to let us help out at his paper so we can learn from the pros how to gather the news and make our own newspaper, the *Nineveh News.*

"We want to make sure everyone knows this incredible story about Jonah. So grab your pens and paper. Molly, get Sam's leash. Let's head downtown so we can get started on our first assignment."

OUR ASSIGNMENT

"Hi, Mr. Davis," Molly announced, "we're here. Uh-oh, Max… you better grab Sam's leash. He just saw Mr. Davis. *Whew!* You got him in the nick of time to save Mr. Davis from a face-licking!"

"Hi, kids." Mr. Davis smiled as he patted Sam's head. "Yes, I have heard all about you too, Sam! Are you ready to get started, Max and Molly?"

"We sure are!"

"Great! Then let's head over to meet Mr. Chase, the head of our editorial department."

"Mr. Chase, this is Max and Molly, and their famous face-licking detective beagle, Sam."

"It's great to meet you. Hi, Sam—I have heard all about you." Mr. Chase chuckled as he reached down to meet Sam.

"Oh, no! He got you!" Max exclaimed. "Sorry about that, Mr. Chase."

"That's okay, Max. I knew he was fast, but not that fast."

The kids started laughing as Sam barked his agreement and wagged his tail.

"Okay, the first thing you need to do to get started on your newspaper is to decide what you want to write about and gather the facts so you can write a great news story," Mr. Chase said.

Guided Instruction

"After you finish writing your story, I will make sure it is accurate before you go to print. Do you guys have a lead on a good front-page story?"

"We sure do!" Max answered. "We are going to investigate the book of Jonah to find out what is happening with one of God's prophets and one of Israel's enemies."

"That sounds like a great lead story," Mr. Chase replied. "Do you know what you need to do first?"

Molly smiled. "We know."

How about you, rookie reporter? Do you know what you need to do before you open your Bible and begin your investigation?

"The first thing you need to do is to talk to God," Mr. Chase reminded them. "The Bible calls this prayer! Bible study should *always* begin with prayer. You need to ask God to be your Master Editor—to direct you by His Holy Spirit so you can understand what the Bible says and handle it accurately."

"Let's pray and ask God for His help as we get ready for our first assignment for the *Nineveh News*," Max said.

They all prayed together.

"I am so proud of you!" Mr. Chase exclaimed. "Now that you have prayed, the next step in becoming a top reporter is to head to the scene and find out what is happening. Good investigative reporters get the *facts*. They know they need to be accurate! Reporters shouldn't go on hunches. Reporters should tell the story just like it happened. That's what we call having *integrity*. Integrity means to be trustworthy and sincere. It means to be honest and to do the right thing even when no one is looking."

Okay, reporters, grab your pencils and let's get the scoop. We are going to begin our investigation by tracking down one of the main characters in our story: *God.*

One way we can uncover clues about main characters is to mark their names in a special way in the Bible so we can get a closer look at these people. Today we are going to mark every place we see the word *God.* We also need to mark each *pronoun* that refers to God. What are pronouns? Check out Mr. Chase's notes.

5

WEEK ONE

10

Pronouns

Pronouns are words that take the place of nouns. A noun is a person, place, or thing. A pronoun stands in for a noun. Look at the two sentences below. Watch how the pronoun *he* is substituted for Max's name in the second sentence.

Max can't wait to track down God because he wants to beat Molly by getting the scoop first.

The word *he* is a pronoun because it takes the place of Max's name in the second sentence. *He* is another word we use to refer to Max.

Watch for these other pronouns when you are marking people's names:

I	you	he	she
me	yours	him	her
mine		his	hers
we	it		
our	its		
they	them		

Now that you know what pronouns are, turn to your Observation Worksheets on page 123. Observation Worksheets have the Bible text printed out for you to use as you study Jonah.

Guided Instruction

5 Turn to page 10 and review "Pronouns."

Guided Instruction

6 Turn to page 123 and read Jonah 1:1–9 aloud as students follow along. If you are teaching in a classroom and have an overhead projector, make a transparency of your Observation Worksheet for a visual aid. You may want to blow it up to poster size and hang it on a wall and then have your students call each key word out loud as you read it and mark it together—you on the transparency and they in their books. If you're skilled at PowerPoint and have time, you can import an Observation Worksheet then select symbols from PP's palette or elsewhere, color them, place them over the words, and even animate them—bring them in one at a time.

God (Lord) (draw a purple triangle and color it yellow)

Stormy Seas   11

Read Jonah 1:1-9 and mark every reference to *God* or LORD in a special way, just like this:

God (LORD—LORD is another name that means God) (draw a purple triangle and color it yellow)

(page 123)

6

OBSERVATION WORKSHEETS

JONAH

Chapter 1

1 The word of the LORD came to Jonah the son of Amittai saying,

2 "Arise, go to Nineveh the great city and cry against it, for their wickedness has come up before Me."

3 But Jonah rose up to flee to Tarshish from the presence of the LORD. So he went down to Joppa, found a ship which was going to Tarshish, paid the fare and went down into it to go with them to Tarshish from the presence of the LORD.

4 The LORD hurled a great wind on the sea and there was a great storm on the sea so that the ship was about to break up.

5 Then the sailors became afraid and every man cried to his god, and they threw the cargo which was in the ship into the sea to lighten it for them. But Jonah had gone below into the hold of the ship, lain down and fallen sound asleep.

6 So the captain approached him and said, "How is it that you are sleeping? Get up, call on your god. Perhaps your god will be concerned about us so that we will not perish."

7 Each man said to his mate, "Come, let us cast lots so we may learn on whose account this calamity has struck us." So they cast lots and the lot fell on Jonah.

8 Then they said to him, "Tell us, now! On whose account has this calamity struck us? What is your occupation? And where do you come from? What is your country? From what people are you?"

9 He said to them, "I am a Hebrew, and I fear the LORD God of heaven who made the sea and the dry land."

10 Then the men became extremely frightened and they said to him,

(page 11)

All right! Now that we have tracked down one of our main subjects of this story, let's find out what we can learn about God from each of these verses. Look at every place you marked *God* (or Lord) on your Observation Worksheet. Make a list in your notebook on what you learned about God (Lord).

7

My List on God

Jonah 1:1 The **word** of the **Lord** came to **Jonah**.

Jonah 1:4 The Lord **hurled** a **great** **wind** on the **sea** and there was a **great** **storm**.

Jonah 1:9 The Lord God of **heaven** who **made** the **sea** and the **dry** **land**.

Wow! WHAT does this list show us about WHO God is and WHAT He can do? In Jonah 1:1 we see that the "Word of the Lord" came to Jonah. This verse shows us that God talks to Jonah. Isn't it awesome to see that God speaks to ordinary people?

In Jonah 1:4, we see the Lord hurls a great wind on the sea

Guided Instruction

7 Complete the list on page 11.

My List on God

Jonah 1:1 The <u>word</u> of the <u>Lord</u> came to <u>Jonah</u>.

Jonah 1:4 The Lord <u>hurled</u> a <u>great</u> <u>wind</u> on the <u>sea</u> and there was a <u>great</u> <u>storm</u>.

Jonah 1:9 The Lord God of <u>heaven</u> who <u>made</u> the <u>sea</u> and the <u>dry</u> <u>land</u>.

Read and discuss the text on pages 11–12.

Guided Instruction

8 Put the missing vowels on each blank to discover your memory verse on page 12.

F o r I k n o w t h a t t h e L ORD i s g r e a t a n d t h a t o u r L ORD i s a b o v e a l l g o d s.

W h a t e v e r t h e L ORD p l e a s e s, H e d o e s, i n h e a v e n a n d o n e a r t h, i n t h e s e a s a n d i n a l l d e e ps.

Psalm 135:5–6

9 Copy the memory verse to an index card and practice saying it three times, three times a day.

---

and causes a great storm. God is all-powerful! He has the power to create storms. He rules over nature!

In Jonah 1:9, we discover that God made the sea and dry land. That shows us that God is *Elohim,* the Creator! He created everything.

Are you blown away at what you have learned about God in these verses today? You know that God talks to people. God is all-powerful. He rules over nature. And God doesn't just rule over nature—He created it. Incredible! Just wait! There is so much more to learn about our awesome God.

We are off and running, but before you leave the office, Mr. Chase has one more assignment for you—your memory verses. Each week you will have a new assignment (one or two Bible verses to learn) to help sharpen your memory skills and give you direction as you do your investigative work.

Max copied down your two verses for this week using his speed-writing skills. Reporters sometimes use speed writing to get the facts down quickly. To decode Max's notes, you need to decide which of the missing vowels (a,e,i,o,u) needs to go on each of the blanks. Put the correct vowel in each blank to discover your memory verses for this week.

8

9

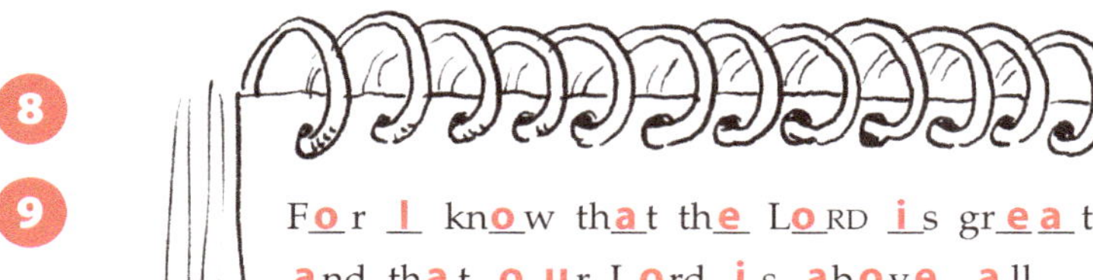

Fantastic! Now look at your verses and write out three things they tell you about God.

10

1. **God is great.**

2. **God is above all gods.**

3. **God does whatever He pleases.**

Name something that has happened in your life or something in the life of someone you know that shows "the LORD is great."

____

____

____

What a day! Did you know these things about God? Why don't you write these verses on an index card? Now practice saying them out loud three times in a row…three times today!

Think about all the wonderful things you learned about God. Wow!

Guided Instruction

10 Write out three things they tell you about God.

1. **God is great.**

2. **God is above all gods.**

3. **God does whatever He pleases.**

Lead a discussion about the next question and have students answer it independently.

Practice saying the memory verse with a friend.

Guided Instruction

DAY TWO

Ask God to give you a clear understanding of His special message to you today.

11 Turn to page 13 and read "A Profile on Jonah."

12 Turn to page 123 and reread Jonah 1:1–9. Use your visual aid as you read out loud to your students. Have them call out every reference to *Jonah* and color it orange as they call it out, marking it together as we noted on page 16.

(page 13)

DAY TWO

11

A PROFILE ON JONAH

It's great to have you back at the office. Mr. Chase has given us our next assignment. Today we need to investigate the other main character in the book of Jonah. Let's get started by talking to our Master Editor and asking for His help as we head back to Israel to dig up the facts on a man named Jonah.

All right! Now that you have prayed, grab those colored pencils and turn to your Observation Worksheet on page 123.

(page 123)

12

OBSERVATION WORKSHEETS

JONAH

Chapter 1

1 The word of the L ORD came to Jonah the son of Amittai saying,

2 "Arise, go to Nineveh the great city and cry against it, for their wickedness has come up before Me."

3 But Jonah rose up to flee to Tarshish from the presence of the L ORD. So he went down to Joppa, found a ship which was going to Tarshish, paid the fare and went down into it to go with them to Tarshish from the presence of the L ORD.

4 The L ORD hurled a great wind on the sea and there was a great storm on the sea so that the ship was about to break up.

5 Then the sailors became afraid and every man cried to his god, and they threw the cargo which was in the ship into the sea to lighten it for them. But Jonah had gone below into the hold of the ship, lain down and fallen sound asleep.

6 So the captain approached him and said, "How is it that you are sleeping? Get up, call on your god. Perhaps your god will be concerned about us so that we will not perish."

7 Each man said to his mate, "Come, let us cast lots so we may learn on whose account this calamity has struck us." So they cast lots and the lot fell on Jonah.

8 Then they said to him, "Tell us, now! On whose account has this calamity struck us? What is your occupation? And where do you come from? What is your country? From what people are you?"

9 He said to them, "I am a Hebrew, and I fear the L ORD God of heaven who made the sea and the dry land."

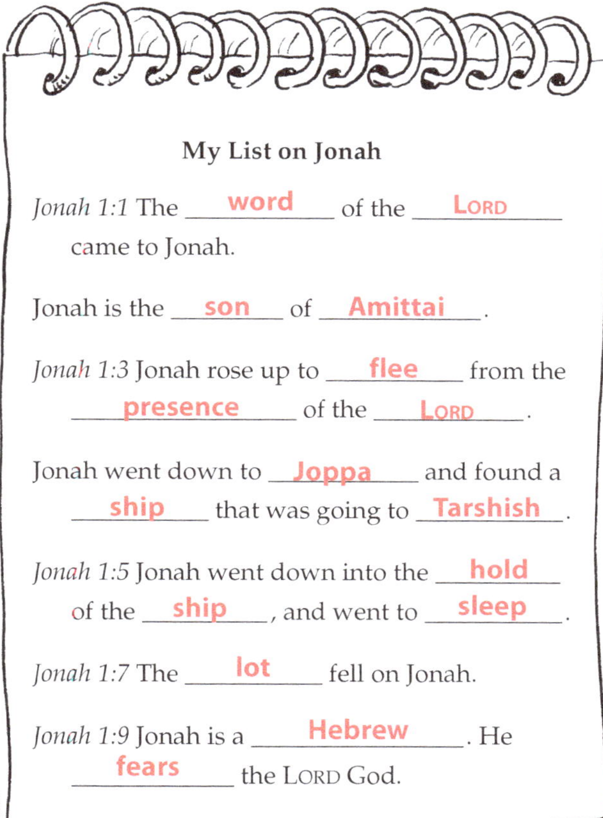

Guided Instruction

13 Make a list on page 14 of what you discover about Jonah.

My List on Jonah

Jonah 1:1 The <u>word</u> of the <u>Lord</u> came to Jonah.

Jonah is the <u>son</u> of <u>Amittai</u>.

Jonah 1:3 Jonah rose up to <u>flee</u> from the <u>presence</u> of the <u>Lord</u>.

Jonah went down to <u>Joppa</u> and found a <u>ship</u> that was going to <u>Tarshish</u>.

Jonah 1:5 Jonah went down into the <u>hold</u> of the <u>ship</u>, and went to <u>sleep</u>.

Jonah 1:7 The <u>lot</u> fell on Jonah.

Jonah 1:9 Jonah is a <u>Hebrew</u>. He <u>fears</u> the Lord God.

Guided Instruction

14 Look up 2 Kings 14:23–25 and answer the following questions.

2 Kings 14:25 WHO is Jonah? **God's servant, the son of Amittai, the prophet**

WHERE is he from? **Gath-hepher**

15 Turn to page 19 and double-underline in green WHERE Jonah is from.

Read the rest of the text on page 15.

Practice saying the memory verse with a friend.

Stormy Seas 15

14   Let's get a little more background information on Jonah by doing some *cross-referencing*. Cross-referencing is where we go to other passages of Scripture and compare Scripture with Scripture. Pull out your Bible and look up 2 Kings 14:23-25.

2 Kings 14:25 WHO is Jonah?

God's servant, the son of Amittai, the prophet

WHERE was he from?   **Gath-hepher**

Turn to page 19 and on the map double-underline in green WHERE Jonah is from. Great investigative work!

(page 19)

15 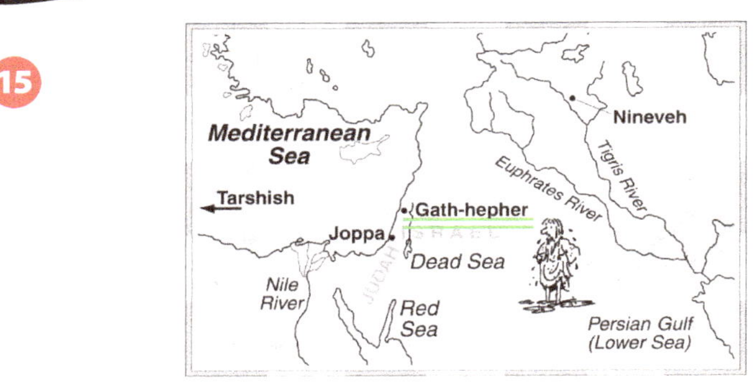

(page 15)

WHERE Jonah is from. Great investigative work!

Now think about the things you have learned about Jonah. You know WHO he is. Jonah is the son of Amittai. He is a Hebrew, which means he is one of God's chosen people—a Jew. He is from Gath-hepher. He is a servant of the Lord—a prophet.

Do you know what a prophet is? A *prophet* is someone who is called by God. God speaks to His prophets through words, visions, and dreams. God's prophet is to tell the people God's words and messages. Some things God wants a prophet to tell the people are what they are doing wrong (sinning) or what God is going to do in the future. Isn't that awesome? Jonah has been called by God to speak His words to other people.

Tomorrow we will continue our research to get more insights into this servant of God. Don't forget to practice your memory verses!

Day

(page 15)

into this servant of God. Don't forget to practice your memory verses!

DAY THREE

GATHER THE FACTS

16 "Okay, kids." Mr. Chase smiled as he looked over Max and

---

16   WEEK ONE

Molly's notebooks. "Your notes are looking good. Your assignment today is to get the facts by asking the 5W's and an H. Every news story always includes the 5W's and an H."

Do you know what the 5 W's and an H are, rookie reporter? They are the WHO, WHAT, WHERE, WHEN, WHY, and HOW questions.

17
1. Asking WHO helps you find out:

   WHO wrote this?

   WHO are we reading about?

   WHO was this passage written to?

   WHO said this or did that?

2. WHAT helps you understand:

   WHAT is the author talking about?

   WHAT are the main things that happen?

3. WHERE helps you learn:

   WHERE did something happen?

   WHERE did they go?

   WHERE was this said?

   When we discover a WHERE, we double-underline the WHERE in green.

4. WHEN tells us about time. We mark it with a green clock or a green circle like this.
   WHEN tells us:

   WHEN did this event happen or WHEN will it happen?

   WHEN did the main characters do something?

   It helps us to follow the order of events.

DAY THREE

God is going to give us an example of what He does when people disobey Him. Ask Him to clarify His Word today.

16 Turn to page 15 and read "Gather the Facts."

17 Review the investigative questions on pages 16-17.

Guided Instruction

18 Turn to page 123 and reread Jonah 1:1–9 to answer questions starting on page 17.

Stormy Seas   17

5. WHY asks questions like:

WHY did he say that?

WHY did they go there?

WHY did this happen?

6. HOW lets you figure out things like:

HOW is something to be done?

HOW did people know something had happened?

Now that you know what the 5 W's and an H are, talk to your Master Editor and ask for His directions so you don't go the wrong way. Great!

Turn to page 123 and read Jonah 1:1-9 again.

(page 123)

OBSERVATION WORKSHEETS

JONAH

18

Chapter 1

1 The word of the LORD came to Jonah the son of Amittai saying,

2 "Arise, go to Nineveh the great city and cry against it, for their wickedness has come up before Me."

3 But Jonah rose up to flee to Tarshish from the presence of the LORD. So he went down to Joppa, found a ship which was going to Tarshish, paid the fare and went down into it to go with them to Tarshish from the presence of the LORD.

4 The LORD hurled a great wind on the sea and there was a great storm on the sea so that the ship was about to break up.

5 Then the sailors became afraid and every man cried to his god, and they threw the cargo which was in the ship into the sea to lighten it for them. But Jonah had gone below into the hold of the ship, lain down and fallen sound asleep.

6 So the captain approached him and said, "How is it that you are sleeping? Get up, call on your god. Perhaps your god will be concerned about us so that we will not perish."

7 Each man said to his mate, "Come, let us cast lots so we may learn on whose account this calamity has struck us." So they cast lots and the lot fell on Jonah.

8 Then they said to him, "Tell us, now! On whose account has this calamity struck us? What is your occupation? And where do you come from? What is your country? From what people are you?"

9 He said to them, "I am a Hebrew, and I fear the LORD God of heaven who made the sea and the dry land."

(page 17)

Okay, rookie reporter, pull out your notebook and start asking the 5 W's and an H.

Jonah 1:1 WHO is the main person in this story?

Jonah

WHAT comes to Jonah?

The Word of the LORD

Remember, that's God speaking to Jonah.

Jonah 1:2 WHAT two things does God tell Jonah to do?

1. **Go to Nineveh.**

2. **Cry out against it.**

18   WEEK ONE

WHY does God want Jonah to cry out against Nineveh?

Because they are wicked

Guided Instruction

Jonah 1:1 WHO is the main person in this story? **Jonah**

WHAT comes to Jonah? **The Word of the LORD**

Jonah 1:2 WHAT two things does God tell Jonah to do?
1. **Go to Nineveh.**
2. **Cry out against it.**

WHY does God want Jonah to cry out against Nineveh? **Because they are wicked**

Guided Instruction

 Read and discuss the notes on Nineveh on page 18.

(page 18)

Take a look at Max and Molly's research notes on Nineveh so you will know what Nineveh was really like.

The Great City of Nineveh

Nineveh was the capital city of the nation of Assyria. Assyria was a longtime enemy of Israel. For more than 100 years, the Assyrians constantly attacked the people in Israel and raided the land.

The Assyrians were fierce warriors who killed or tortured the people they defeated, and that included the Jews (God's chosen people).

Nineveh was a very large city. In fact, it took three days to walk through it. It was located on the east bank of the Tigris River. It was built at the main river crossing leading to the best farm-land. The wall that surrounded the city was 50 feet high.

Nineveh was also home to many beautiful temples built to honor and worship false gods. The people's worship of idols (false gods) made God very angry.

Today, the ruins of Nineveh are found in Iraq, across the Tigris River from the modern-day city of Mosul.

OBSERVATION WORKSHEETS

JONAH

(page 123)

Chapter 1

1 The word of the LORD came to Jonah the son of Amittai saying,

2 "Arise, go to Nineveh the great city and cry against it, for their wickedness has come up before Me."

3 But Jonah rose up to flee to Tarshish from the presence of the LORD. So he went down to Joppa, found a ship which was going to Tarshish, paid the fare and went down into it to go with them to Tarshish from the presence of the LORD.

4 The LORD hurled a great wind on the sea and there was a great storm on the sea so that the ship was about to break up.

5 Then the sailors became afraid and every man cried to his god, and they threw the cargo which was in the ship into the sea to lighten it for them. But Jonah had gone below into the hold of the ship, lain down and fallen sound asleep.

6 So the captain approached him and said, "How is it that you are sleeping? Get up, call on your god. Perhaps your god will be concerned about us so that we will not perish."

7 Each man said to his mate, "Come, let us cast lots so we may learn on whose account this calamity has struck us." So they cast lots and the lot fell on Jonah.

8 Then they said to him, "Tell us, now! On whose account has this calamity struck us? What is your occupation? And where do you come from? What is your country? From what people are you?"

9 He said to them, "I am a Hebrew, and I fear the LORD God of heaven who made the sea and the dry land."

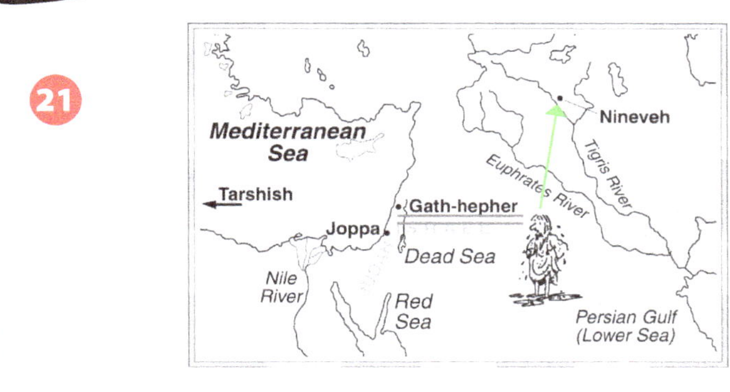

Guided Instruction

20 Turn to page 123 and double-underline the word that answers WHERE on the Observation Sheet.

21 On the map on page 19 draw a green arrow from Jonah to WHERE God told him to go.

Guided Instruction

Jonah 1:2 WHERE does God want Jonah to go? To Nineveh

Jonah 1:3 WHERE did Jonah go to find a ship? Joppa

Double-underline this WHERE in green on your Observation Worksheet on page 123.

22 Turn to page 19 and draw a RED ARROW from Jonah to Joppa.

Jonah 1:2 WHERE does God want Jonah to go?

To Nineveh

When we discover a WHERE in the Bible, we double-underline the WHERE in green. Turn to page 123 and double-underline in green the word that tells WHERE on your Observation Worksheet in Jonah 1:2.

Now look at the map and draw a green arrow from Jonah to WHERE God told him to go.

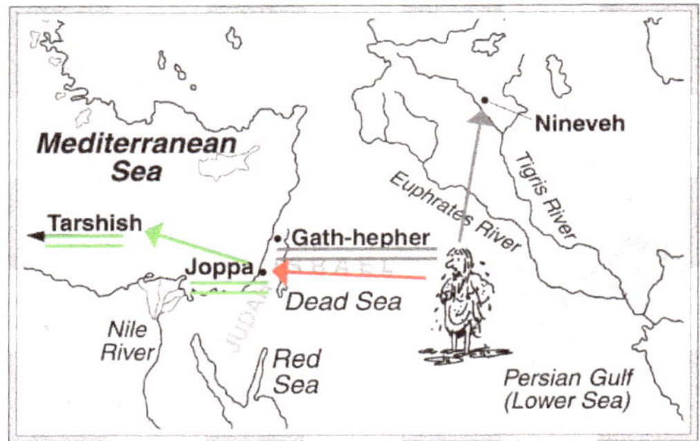

Wow! Are you surprised that God wanted Jonah to go and tell these people, who were Israel's enemy, what they were doing wrong?

Jonah 1:3 WHERE did Jonah go to find a ship?

Joppa

Double-underline this WHERE in green on your Observation Worksheet on page 123.

Look back at your map and draw a red arrow from Jonah to WHERE he went to find a ship.

20   WEEK ONE

Jonah 1:3 WHERE is the ship going? WHERE does Jonah want to go? **Tarshish**

Double-underline this WHERE in green. Then look at your map and draw another arrow from Joppa to WHERE the ship was going to take Jonah.

Is this where God told Jonah to go? ____ Yes **X** No

Is Jonah going the right way or the wrong way? **Wrong way**

Jonah 1:3 HOW did Jonah respond to God's command?

He fled to **Tarshish** from the p **r e s e n c** e of the L **O R** D.

Can you do that? Can you run away from God? ____ Yes **X** No How do you know? Let's find out. Look up and read Psalm 139:1-10 in your Bible.

Psalm 139:2 WHAT do we see about the LORD?

"You know when I ___**sit**___ down and when I ___**rise**___ up; You **understand** my ___**thought**___ from afar."

Psalm 139:7-10 Can you get away from God's Spirit or flee from His presence? ____ Yes **X** No

Isn't God amazing? God knows your thoughts. And there isn't any place you can go to get away from His presence. Jonah is headed in the opposite direction from where God told him to go. He is trying to run away from God, but God is still with

Guided Instruction

Jonah 1:3 WHERE is the ship going? WHERE does Jonah want to go? **Tarshish**

23 Double-underline Tarshish in green. On the map, draw another arrow from Joppa to this city WHERE the ship was going to take Jonah.

Is this where God told Jonah to go? **No**

Is Jonah going the right way or the wrong way? **Wrong way**

Jonah 1:3 HOW did Jonah respond to God's command? **He fled to Tarshish from the p r e s e n c e of the L O R D.**

Lead a discussion about running away from God.

Read Psalm 139:1–10

Psalm 139:2 WHAT do we see about the LORD? **"You know when I sit down and when I rise up; You understand my thought from afar."**

Psalm 139:7–10 Can you get away from God's Spirit or flee from His presence? **No**

Lead a discussion.

Guided Instruction

Read and discuss the questions on page 21 and have students respond independently.

Practice saying the memory verse with a friend.

---

him. God told Jonah what to do, but Jonah has chosen to do the wrong thing.

HOW about you, rookie reporter? Can you think of a time when you knew the right thing to do but didn't do it? Write out a brief story about WHAT you did, WHAT happened, and WHAT you should have done.

Wrong Way, _______________________!
(put your name here)

____

____

____

____

____

Way to go! WHAT will you do the next time something like that happens?

____

Good for you! Now don't forget to practice your memory verses.

Tomorrow we will hop on the boat with Jonah to find out what happens next.

(page 21)

what happens next.

24

MORE RESEARCH

Watch out! Here comes Sam. He is so excited about being on the trail of a hot news story. Look at him sniffing around. Quick!

Give him a treat so we can continue to get the facts now that we know Jonah has chosen to go the wrong way, going to Tarshish instead of to Nineveh like God told him to do. We need to find out what happens. Don't forget to pray!

Let's head back to the book of Jonah and continue our investigation by marking key words. What are *key words?* Key words are words that pop up more than once. They are called key words because they help unlock the meaning of the chapter or book you are studying and give you clues about what is most important in a passage of Scripture.

25

✓ Key words are usually used over and over again. (That's because God doesn't want you to miss the point.)

✓ Key words are important.

✓ Key words are used by the writer for a reason.

Once you discover a key word, you need to mark it in a special way using a special color or symbol so that you can immediately spot it in Scripture.

You may also want to make a bookmark for these key words so you can know what they are at a glance as you mark them on your Observation Worksheets.

To make a key-word bookmark, get an index card or a piece of

Ask God to help you reflect on your obedience to Him. He will guide you to full understanding so that you will not fall into the trap Jonah did.

24 Turn to page 21 and read "More Research."

25 Review key words and synonyms on pages 22–23

Guided Instruction

paper and write the key words we've listed, as well as how you are going to mark them on your Observation Worksheets.

When you mark your key words, you will also need to mark any other words that mean the same thing, such as pronouns and synonyms. (You learned what pronouns were when you marked *God* and *Jonah.*) Take a look at Max and Molly's notebook to learn about synonyms.

Synonyms

Synonyms are different words that mean the same thing. For example, *sailboat, yacht,* and *rowboat* are different words, but they are all names of types of boats. That's a synonym—it says the same thing but with a different word.

Great! Turn to page 123. Read Jonah 1:1-9 and mark the key words and any synonyms for those words that we have listed for you.

Key Words

storm (calamity) (draw a blue wavy line under the word and red lines like this over the word and color the word red)

sailors (color it blue)

pray (cried, call) (draw a purple and color it pink)

captain (color it red)

Don't forget to mark the pronouns! And mark anything that

tells you WHEN by drawing a green clock or green circle like this: .

Get the facts. Find out WHAT happens after Jonah gets on

(page 123)

OBSERVATION WORKSHEETS
JONAH

26 **Chapter 1**

1 The word of the LORD came to Jonah the son of Amittai saying,

2 "Arise, go to Nineveh the great city and cry against it, for their wickedness has come up before Me."

3 But Jonah rose up to flee to Tarshish from the presence of the LORD. So he went down to Joppa, found a ship which was going to Tarshish, paid the fare and went down into it to go with them to Tarshish from the presence of the LORD.

4 The LORD hurled a great wind on the sea and there was a great storm on the sea so that the ship was about to break up.

5 Then the sailors became afraid and every man cried to his god, and they threw the cargo which was in the ship into the sea to lighten it for them. But Jonah had gone below into the hold of the ship, lain down and fallen sound asleep.

6 So the captain approached him and said, "How is it that you are sleeping? Get up, call on your god. Perhaps your god will be concerned about us so that we will not perish."

7 Each man said to his mate, "Come, let us cast lots so we may learn on whose account this calamity has struck us." So they cast lots and the lot fell on Jonah.

8 Then they said to him, "Tell us, now! On whose account has this calamity struck us? What is your occupation? And where do you come from? What is your country? From what people are you?"

9 He said to them, "I am a Hebrew, and I fear the LORD God of heaven who made the sea and the dry land."

(page 24)

Get the facts. Find out WHAT happens after Jonah gets on board the ship. Ask those 5W's and an H.

27 Jonah 1:4 WHAT did the Lord do when Jonah tried to run from His presence?

He hurled a great wind on the sea.

Jonah 1:5 HOW did the sailors respond to the storm?

They became afraid and called on their gods.

Did their gods answer? **No**

Look at WHAT the sailors did next.

WHAT did the sailors do after they cried to their gods?

They threw cargo overboard.

Guided Instruction

26 Have your students make a key word bookmark by copying the key words on an index card, or write them on the whiteboard in your classroom. Turn to page 123 and read Jonah 1:1–9 aloud using your visual aid as your students or child follows along. Have your students call each key word out loud as you read it, then mark it together, you on your visual aid and they in their books.

Storm, calamity (draw a blue wavy line under the word and red lines over the word and color it red)

Sailors (color it blue)

Pray (cried, call) (draw a purple bowl and color it pink)

Captain (color it red)

Mark pronouns.

WHEN (draw a green clock over words that denote time)

27 Reread the selected verses to answer the questions.

Jonah 1:4 WHAT did the Lord do when Jonah tried to run from His presence? He hurled a great wind on the sea.

Jonah 1:5 HOW did the sailor respond to the storm? They became afraid and called on their gods.

DID their gods answer? No

WHAT did the sailors do next? They threw cargo overboard.

Guided Instruction

WHAT was Jonah doing? Sleeping

Jonah 1:6 WHAT are the captain's instructions to Jonah? Get up, call on your god.

Jonah 1:7 WHAT do the sailors do to find out why this calamity has struck them? They cast lots.

Jonah 1:4 WHAT calamity did they face? HOW is it described? A great storm

(page 24)

WHAT is Jonah doing?

Sleeping

Stormy Seas   25

Jonah 1:6 WHAT are the captain's instructions to Jonah?

Get up, call on your god.

Jonah 1:7 WHAT do the sailors do to find out why this calamity has struck them?

They cast lots.

Do you know what a *calamity* is? A calamity is deep trouble or misery. It can be anything that brings great loss or disaster.

WHAT is the calamity the sailors face? HOW is it described in Jonah 1:4?

A great storm

(page 25)

The calamity in Jonah 1 was the storm. Did you mark *storm* and *calamity* the same way?

Since the sailors cast lots to find out who was causing this calamity, let's look at Max and Molly's notes to find out what it means to cast lots.

28

Casting Lots

In the Old Testament, people cast lots to decide things. God sometimes used these lots to reveal truth to His people. Lots were small bits of wood or stone. Sometimes the names of people were written on the stones. The stones were placed in a container and shaken together. The first "lot" to fall out showed who was chosen.

W E E K   O N E

Jonah 1:7 WHO did the lot fall on? **Jonah**

Wow! The storm (the calamity) happened because of Jonah.

Jonah 1:8 WHAT did the sailors want to know about Jonah?

Why has this happened? What is your occupation? Where are you from? What is your country? Who are your people?

Jonah 1:9 WHAT did Jonah say?

I am a Hebrew and I fear the Lord God of heaven.

Look back at Jonah 1:2. WHAT didn't Jonah tell them?

God told me to go to Nineveh.

What a story! Can you believe it? God sent this terrifying storm because Jonah disobeyed Him. WHAT lessons do you learn for your life?

____

____

affected

---

28 Read the note "Casting Lots" on page 25.

Jonah 1:7 WHO did the lot fall on?
Jonah

Jonah 1:8 WHAT did the sailors want to know about Jonah? Why has this happened? What is your occupation? Where are you from? What is your country? Who are your people?

Jonah 1:9 WHAT did Jonah say? I am a Hebrew and I fear the Lord God of heaven.

Jonah 1:2 WHAT didn't Jonah tell them? God told me to go to Nineveh.

What lesson can you learn for your life? Answer independently.

Guided Instruction

WHO else is affected on the ship? <u>The sailors and the captain</u>

29 Read and discuss the questions on pages 27-28 and respond independently.

(page 26)

Think about the storm God sent. Is Jonah the only one affected by this storm?

  ____ Yes **X** No

WHO else is affected on the ship?

The sailors and the captain

  Think about these other people. The sailors are afraid. They throw the cargo overboard to lighten the ship. The captain is responsible for the cargo that is now lost.

  Do you see how Jonah's disobedience affected other people? When you sin, it doesn't just affect you. When you sin you also

---

Stormy Seas 27

29

hurt other people. Can you think of a time when you did something wrong and it hurt someone else? Write out WHAT you did and WHAT happened.

____

____

  Jonah says he fears God in verse 9. To fear God is to know God, to trust God, and to respect God. If God tells you to do something, if you fear Him then you listen and obey Him. Does Jonah really fear God since he is disobeying and running away?

____

____

  Does Jonah think he can get away with this? __________

  How about you? Have you ever thought you could do something wrong and you wouldn't get caught?

    ____ Yes ____ No

WHAT was it? WHAT happened?

____

____

  Do you listen to what God tells you in His Word and obey Him?

    ____ Yes ____ No ____ Sometimes

Write out one way you obey God.

____

  The sailors questioned who Jonah was because he was the reason for the storm. Can people tell you are a Christian by watching you? Or does the way you behave cause others to have doubts about you? For instance…

28   WEEK ONE

- Do you help others? Name one way you helped someone else.

  ____

- Do you watch things you shouldn't watch on TV, at the movies, or on the Internet?

  ____ Yes ____ No ____ Sometimes

- HOW do you speak to your parents and teachers—with respect or with disrespect?

  ____

- Are you kind to kids who don't have any friends? Circle the answer that best fits you.

  a. No—I have my own special friends that I hang out with.

  b. Sometimes—it depends on my friends and who the kid is.

  c. Yes—I am friendly and talk to kids who don't have any friends. I invite them to hang out with me.

If your answer was *no* or *sometimes*, change your actions by being kind to someone this week.

From the way you answered all the questions, do your actions show others that you know God?

  ____ Yes ____ No

Write out WHAT you need to change if your actions don't show you love and obey God.

  ____

  ____

All right! You did a fantastic job uncovering the story and applying what you learned to your life. Now don't forget to practice your memory verses!

Guided Instruction

Practice saying the memory verse.

Guided Instruction

Ask God to give you direction in this lesson. Ask Him to help you identify important points to write the story.

30 Turn to page 29 and read "The Deadline Approaches" and "Writing the Story."

30

THE DEADLINE APPROACHES

"Wow!" Max said to Molly. "I am sooooo excited about all we have uncovered for our first news story. Look at what we have discovered about God, Jonah, and what is happening on the ship. Were you surprised that Jonah's actions affected everybody on the ship?"

"I sure was. I never thought about that before. Isn't it cool that God isn't just using this assignment so we can get a great news story? God is going to use it to teach us how we should live and how important it is for us to obey Him."

"But we better hurry," Max replied. "Mr. Chase needs to look at our copy today. We need to talk to God and get on this assignment right away."

All right! Now that we have prayed, let's get started. Mr. Chase needs you to write your story so we can go to print. Turn to page 123 and read Jonah 1:1-9.

WRITING THE STORY

(page 123)

OBSERVATION WORKSHEETS

JONAH

Chapter 1

1 The word of the LORD came to Jonah the son of Amittai saying,

2 "Arise, go to Nineveh the great city and cry against it, for their wickedness has come up before Me."

3 But Jonah rose up to flee to Tarshish from the presence of the LORD. So he went down to Joppa, found a ship which was going to Tarshish, paid the fare and went down into it to go with them to Tarshish from the presence of the LORD.

4 The LORD hurled a great wind on the sea and there was a great storm on the sea so that the ship was about to break up.

5 Then the sailors became afraid and every man cried to his god, and they threw the cargo which was in the ship into the sea to lighten it for them. But Jonah had gone below into the hold of the ship, lain down and fallen sound asleep.

6 So the captain approached him and said, "How is it that you are sleeping? Get up, call on your god. Perhaps your god will be concerned about us so that we will not perish."

7 Each man said to his mate, "Come, let us cast lots so we may learn on whose account this calamity has struck us." So they cast lots and the lot fell on Jonah.

8 **Then** **they** said to **him**, "Tell **us**, now! On whose account has this **calamity** struck **us**? What is **your** occupation? And where do **you** come from? What is **your** country? From what people are **you**?"

9 **He** said to them, "**I** am a Hebrew, and **I** fear the LORD God of heaven who made the sea and the dry land."

(page 29)

WRITING THE STORY

The first thing you need to do when writing is to get the readers' attention. That means you need a good headline. A good headline is short. It lets the reader know what the story is about in just a few words. It also needs to grab the reader's attention.

Think about the main thing that happened in Jonah 1:1-9 and write a headline—a few words that describe the main event—at the top of the newspaper on page 30.

WHAT is the weather like, according to Jonah 1:1-9? To make your story even more eye-catching, draw a picture in the weather box on page 30 to show what the weather is like while they are at sea. Then write the story by filling in the blanks on the newspaper.

Oh, and don't forget: Every great news story needs a picture that captures the event for readers. During the time in history

Guided Instruction

31 Transfer the format of "Nineveh News Issue 1" to chart-size paper. As students reread Jonah 1:1–9 fill in the chart on page 30.

NINEVEH NEWS

ISSUE 1

BREAKING NEWS!

(headline) **Jonah Thrown Overboard!**

WEATHER:

STORMY (draw a picture)

Jonah was commanded by **God** to go to **Nineveh** to **cry** out against it. (**DRAW A PICTURE**) But sources say Jonah fled from **God** by going to **Joppa** to get on a ship headed to **Tarshish**.

Not long after the ship set sail, the **Lord** sent a great **wind**. (storm)

As the waves crashed overboard, the sailors threw the cargo overboard to save the ship. The captain woke Jonah up and told him to call on his God. The sailors decided to cast **lots** to find out why this **calamity** had struck. When the lot fell on **Jonah**, the sailors asked him many questions. Jonah told them, "I am a Hebrew, and I fear the **Lord God** of heaven who made the sea and dry land."

---

30   WEEK ONE

that Jonah lived, they didn't have cameras so they had to draw pictures. Draw a picture in the box on your newspaper to show the main event that happens in Jonah 1:1-9. You need just the right shot to get your readers' attention.

31

NINEVEH NEWS

ISSUE 1

BREAKING NEWS!

STORMY
(draw a picture)
Weather

Jonah Thrown Overboard!
(Put your headline here)

_____ **Jonah** _____ was commanded
WHO (Jonah 1:1)

by **God** to go to _____ **Nineveh** _____
WHOM (Jonah 1:1)   WHERE (Jonah 1:2)

to _____ **cry** _____ out against it.
WHAT (Jonah 1:2)

But sources say Jonah fled from

God by going to _____ **Joppa** _____
WHOM (Jonah 1:3)   WHERE (Jonah 1:3)

to get on a ship headed to

_____ **Tarshish** _____ .
WHERE (Jonah 1:3)

Not long after the ship set

sail, the _____ **Lord** _____ sent a great
WHO (Jonah 1:4)

_____ **wind** _____ . (storm)
WHAT (Jonah 1:4)

As the waves crashed over-

board, the sailors threw the cargo

overboard to save the ship. The

captain woke Jonah up and told

him to call on his God. The sailors

DRAW A PICTURE

decided to cast _____ **lots** _____ to find
WHAT (Jonah 1:7)

out why this _____ **calamity** _____ had
WHAT (Jonah 1:7)

struck. When the lot fell on

_____ **Jonah** _____ , the sailors asked
WHOM (Jonah 1:7)

him many questions. Jonah told

them, "I am a Hebrew, and I fear

the _____ **Lord** _____ **God** _____ of heaven
WHOM (Jonah 1:9)

who made the sea and dry land."

Stormy Seas 31

Congratulations! We are ready to print!

You have just published your first edition of the *Nineveh News*. What a story! Our readers can't wait to find out what happens next.

Now, say your memory verses out loud to a grown-up.

WHAT evidence did you see in Jonah 1:1-9 that the LORD God does as He pleases?

Isn't God awesome?

"EXTRA! EXTRA!"

Mr. Davis is so proud of all your hard work at writing your first newspaper story that he would like to give you a bonus—something extra that is fun to do. That's why we call it "Extra! Extra!"

Why don't you act out your amazing news story for your friends, family, school, or church? Max and Molly are acting out their story with the kids at church. They want to share some of their creative ideas with you. You can use some of their ideas or come up with your own to act out your story.

Max and Molly's Ideas

Make two signs like arrows—one to point the way to Nineveh and one for Tarshish. Use a rubber boat, a small swimming pool, or a big cardboard box for your ship. Get some medium cardboard boxes or shoe boxes to use as cargo on the ship.

You can use a blue plastic tablecloth for your stormy sea. Have two kids stand at each end of the plastic tablecloth and snap and wiggle it to imitate the storm.

WHAT will the rain sound like?

HOW can you make the wind noises?

Wake Jonah up and cast lots by putting some rocks in a cup and shaking them until one falls out to discover who is causing the storm.

Be creative and have fun!

Guided Instruction

Say the memory verse aloud to a grown-up.

WHAT evidence did you see in Jonah 1:1–9 that the Lord God does as He pleases? Lead a discussion.

32 Read "EXTRA! EXTRA!" And "Max and Molly's Ideas" on page 31.

Set up a station in the room to complete the project.

Good job! God notices your perseverance and is pleased.

If you are a classroom teacher you may want to give your students a quiz on their memory verse. There is also a quiz on Week One on page 138 to check the memory and understanding.

If you are a Sunday School teacher this is a great time to review the whole week by playing a game like *M&M® Draw* on page 148.

Guided Instruction

WEEK 2

What do you think God will do if you continue to disobey Him? Ask Him to keep your mind on Him and to give you a special message today.

33 Turn to page 32–33 and read "Man Overboard!" and "Back to the Ship."

2

JONAH 1:10-17

Hi, guys! It's great to have you back at the newspaper. Are you ready for another exciting week? As we went to print with our first edition of the *Nineveh News*, we saw that Jonah was in quite a mess. God has given Jonah a message to tell the people in Nineveh, but instead of heading to Nineveh to deliver God's message, Jonah hops on a boat going in the opposite direction.

What does God do to this disobedient prophet who thinks he can run away? He sends a great storm that is about to break up the ship. What will happen next? Will the ship be destroyed? Will the sailors and Jonah drown? How will God get this "wrong way" prophet's complete attention? Let's find out.

33

BACK TO THE SHIP

"Hey, Molly, grab our notebooks while I put Sam on his leash. We have to go back to the scene in Jonah 1. We need to find out WHAT is happening with the storm raging all around the ship Jonah is on."

32

Man Overboard!   33

"I've got them, Max," Molly replied. "Let's pray first. Okay, now we're ready to go."

All right! Now that you've talked to God, let's track the main characters and events. Turn to page 123. Read Jonah 1:10-17 and mark the following key words, any synonyms, and the key phrase on your Observation Worksheets.

A key phrase is like a key word except it is a *group* of words that are repeated instead of just one word. Look at the key words. The group of words "from the presence of the Lord" is a key phrase that is repeated.

LORD or God (draw a purple triangle and color it yellow)

Jonah (color it orange)

from the presence of the LORD (underline it in purple)

great storm (the sea was becoming increasingly stormy, the sea was becoming even stormier) (draw a blue wavy line under the words and red lines like this over the words and color the words red)

men (color it blue) (WHO are these men? If you follow the pronouns back to verse 5, you will see that these men are the sailors.)

pray (called) (draw a purple and color it pink)

appointed (color it green)

Don't forget to mark your pronouns! And mark anything that tells you WHEN by drawing a green clock or a green circle like this .

Oh no! The wind has grabbed Molly's notebook and ripped her pages out so that this week's memory verses are all mixed up.

Guided Instruction

 **34** Add new key words to bookmark. Turn to page 123 and read Jonah 1:10–17 aloud as students follow along and call out each key word as you mark them together as we noted on page 16.

Lord, God (draw a purple triangle and color it yellow)

Jonah (color it orange)

From the presence of the Lord (underline it in purple)

The sea was becoming increasingly stormy. (draw a blue wavy line under the words and red squiggly lines over the words and color the words red)

Great storm (draw a blue wavy line under the words and red squiggly lines over the words and color the words red)

Men (color it blue)

Pray (called) (draw a purple bowl and color it pink)

Appointed (color it green)

WHEN (draw a green clock over words that denote time)

Copy the new words to the bookmark.

---

who made the sea and the dry land."

34 10 Then the men became extremely frightened and they said to him, "How could you do this?" For the men knew that he was fleeing from the presence of the Lord, because he had told them.

123

---

124   *Observation Worksheets*

11 So they said to him, "What should we do to you that the sea may become calm for us?"—for the sea was becoming increasingly stormy.

12 He said to them, "Pick me up and throw me into the sea. Then the sea will become calm for you, for I know that on account of me this great storm has come upon you."

13 However, the men rowed desperately to return to land but they could not, for the sea was becoming even stormier against them.

14 Then they called on the Lord and said, "We earnestly pray, O Lord, do not let us perish on account of this man's life and do not put innocent blood on us; for You, O Lord, have done as You have pleased."

15 So they picked up Jonah, threw him into the sea, and the sea stopped its raging.

16 Then the men feared the Lord greatly, and they offered a sacrifice to the Lord and made vows.

17 And the Lord appointed a great fish to swallow Jonah, and Jonah was in the stomach of the fish three days and three nights.

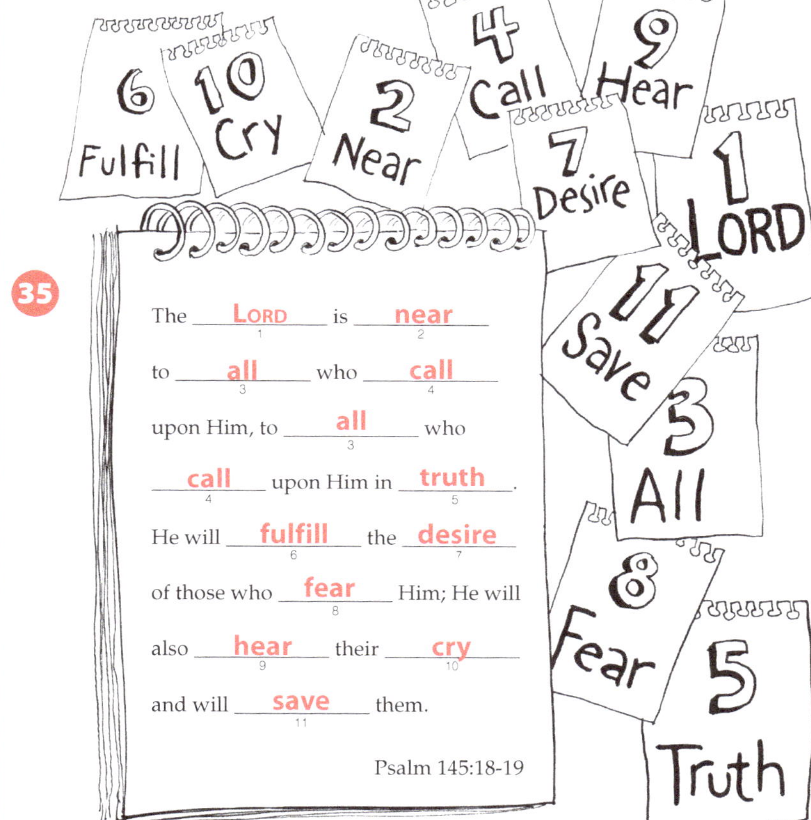

35 Write the word on each piece of paper on the line that matches the numbers to discover this week's verses.

Now write these verses on an index card and practice saying
them three times in a row out loud, three times today! Don't
forget: Reporters need great memory skills.

35 Turn to page 34 and fill in the blanks to find the memory verse.

The <u>Lord</u> is <u>near</u> to <u>all</u> who <u>call</u> upon Him, to <u>all</u> who <u>call</u> upon Him in <u>truth</u>. He will <u>fulfill</u> the <u>desire</u> of those who <u>fear</u> Him; He will also <u>hear</u> their <u>cry</u> and will <u>save</u> them.

Psalm 145:18–19

Copy the memory verse to an index card and practice saying it three times, three times a day.

Guided Instruction

DAY
TWO

Ask God to enlighten your mind today so that you will have a clear understanding of His Word.

36 Turn to page 35 and read "Gather the Facts."

37 Turn to page 123 and reread Jonah 1:9–17 to answer the questions.

DAY
TWO

36

GATHER THE FACTS

Grab your notebook, rookie reporter. You need to get back to the ship and find out WHAT is happening as this storm rages so you can inform your readers. Don't forget to pray and ask your Master Editor for His help.

All right! Turn to page 123. Read Jonah 1:9-17. Let's ask those 5 W's and an H.

---

who made the sea and the dry land."

37 10 Then the men became extremely frightened and they said to him, "How could you do this?" For the men knew that he was fleeing from the presence of the LORD, because he had told them.

123

---

11 So they said to him, "What should we do to you that the sea may become calm for us?"—for the sea was becoming increasingly stormy.

12 He said to them, "Pick me up and throw me into the sea. Then the sea will become calm for you, for I know that on account of me this great storm has come upon you."

13 However, the men rowed desperately to return to land but they could not, for the sea was becoming even stormier against them.

14 Then they called on the LORD and said, "We earnestly pray, O LORD, do not let us perish on account of this man's life and do not put innocent blood on us; for You, O LORD, have done as You have pleased."

15 So they picked up Jonah, threw him into the sea, and the sea stopped its raging.

16 Then the men feared the LORD greatly, and they offered a sacrifice to the LORD and made vows.

17 And the LORD appointed a great fish to swallow Jonah, and Jonah was in the stomach of the fish three days and three nights.

Chapter 2

(page 35)

Jonah 1:10 WHAT do we see about the men when they find out who Jonah is and that he is fleeing from God?

They are extremely _____**frightened**_____.

HOW did the men know that Jonah was fleeing from the presence of the Lord? _____**Jonah**_____ told them.

Jonah 1:11 WHAT are the weather conditions? WHAT do we see about the sea?

The sea was becoming increasingly _____**stormy**_____.

Jonah 1:12 WHAT did Jonah tell the men to do to calm the sea?

"Pick me up and ___**throw**___ me into the ___**sea**___."

Jonah 1:13 WHAT did the men do?

The men **rowed** desperately to return to **land**.

---

36   WEEK TWO

WHAT do we see about the weather now?

The sea was becoming even _____**stormier**_____ against them.

Jonah 1:14 WHAT did the men do?

They _____**called**_____ on the _____**LORD**_____.

WHAT did the sailors pray?

"We earnestly pray, O LORD, do not let us _____**perish**_____ on account of this man's _____**life**_____ and do not put innocent _____**blood**_____ on us; for You, O LORD have done as You have pleased."

Jonah 1:15 WHAT did they do after they prayed?

They picked up Jonah and _____**threw**_____ him into the ___**sea**___.

Guided Instruction

Jonah 1:10 WHAT do we see about the men when they find out who Jonah is and that he is fleeing from God? They are extremely <u>frightened</u>.

HOW did the men know that Jonah was fleeing from the presence of the Lord? <u>Jonah</u> told them.

Jonah 1:11 WHAT are the weather conditions? WHAT do we see about the sea? The sea was becoming increasingly <u>stormy</u>.

Jonah 1:12 WHAT did Jonah tell the men to do to calm the sea? "Pick me up and <u>throw</u> me into the <u>sea</u>."

Jonah 1:13 WHAT did the men do? The men <u>rowed</u> desperately to return to <u>land</u>.

WHAT do you see about the weather now? The sea was becoming even <u>stormier</u> against them.

Jonah 1:14 WHAT did the men do? They <u>called</u> on the LORD.

WHAT did the sailors pray? "We earnestly pray, O LORD, do not let us <u>perish</u> on account of this man's <u>life</u> and do not put innocent <u>blood</u> on us; for You, O Lord have done as You pleased."

Jonah 1:15 WHAT did they do after they prayed? They picked up Jonah and <u>threw</u> him into the <u>sea</u>.

Guided Instruction

WHAT happened to the sea? The sea stopped its raging.

Jonah 1:16 WHAT do we see about the sailors? They feared the Lord greatly.

WHAT did they do? The offered a sacrifice to the Lord and made vows.

Jonah 1:17 WHAT did the Lord do? The Lord appointed a great fish to swallow Jonah.

WHERE is Jonah? In the stomach of the fish

HOW long was Jonah there? Three days and three nights

38 Read the text at the bottom of page 37.

(page 36)

WHAT happened to the sea?

The sea ___stopped___ its raging.

Jonah 1:16 WHAT do we see about the sailors?

They ___feared___ the Lord greatly.

WHAT did they do?

They offered a ___sacrifice___ to the Lord and made ___vows___ .

Man Overboard!   37

Jonah 1:17 WHAT did the Lord do?

The Lord ___appointed___ a ___great___ ___fish___ to swallow Jonah.

WHERE is Jonah?

In the ___stomach___ of the ___fish___

HOW long was Jonah there?

___Three___ ___days___ and ___three___ ___nights___

38 Incredible! The storm continues to get worse, and Jonah tells the sailors to throw him overboard. The sailors call on God and are saved. But WHERE does Jonah end up? In the stomach of a fish! Can you believe that? God could have let Jonah drown, but what did our awesome God do? He appointed a great fish to swallow Jonah! *Appointed* means God picked this fish out and sent it to swallow Jonah. Isn't God powerful? That is pretty amazing!

Mr. Chase thinks we need a puzzle for our paper. Look at the word search and make sure it is ready to print. Find the words from the blanks in the questions you just answered for Day Two, and circle them in the word search. If a word is used more than once, you only have to find and circle it in the puzzle one time.

All right! You are closing in on another story. Don't forget to practice your memory verses.

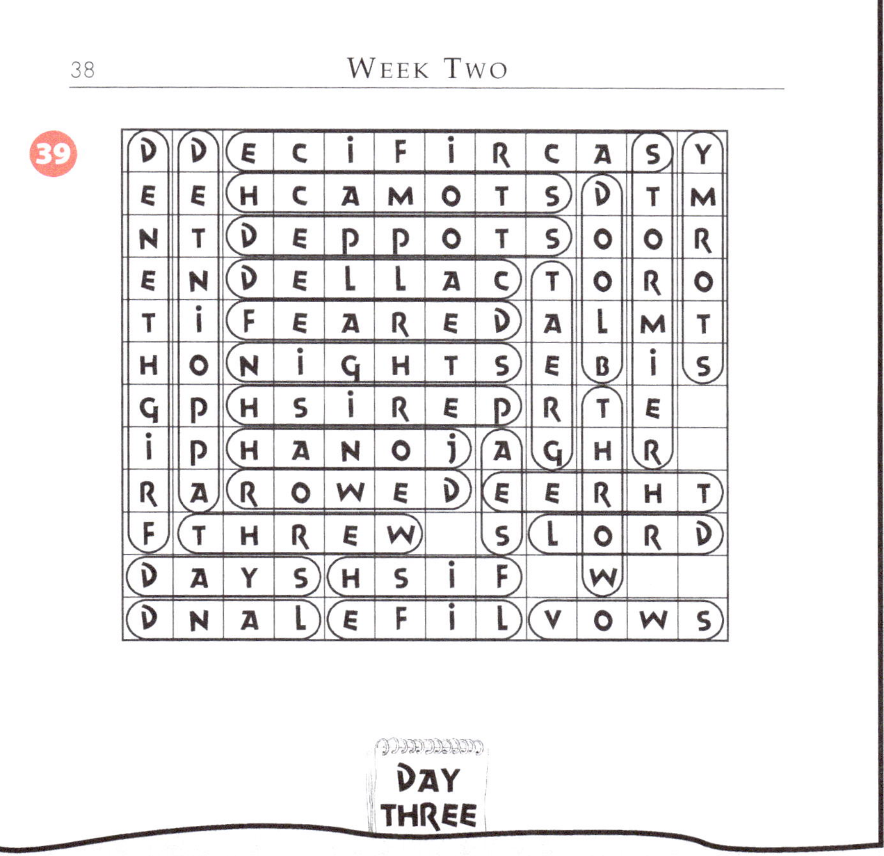

Guided Instruction

39 Complete the word search on page 38.

Practice saying the memory verse with a friend.

Guided Instruction

Ask God to keep your eyes on Him so that you will understand His Word.

40 Turn to page 38 and read "Profile the Characters."

41 Turn to page 123 and reread Jonah 1:10–17.

(page 38)

40

PROFILE THE CHARACTERS

"Quick, Max! Grab Sam. He has my notebook," Molly cried out as she chased Sam around the newsroom.

Max came around the other side of the desk. "Gotcha!" he said as he stopped Sam. Sam released the book and wagged his tail.

"You are one bad dog!" Molly said, exasperated. "What are we

Man Overboard!   39

going to do with you?" Sam jumped up, barked, and licked Molly smack in the face. "Ahhhhh, Sam—yuck!"

Max and Mr. Chase cracked up laughing. "Okay, Sam. That's enough. Time to get back to work," Max said. "Mr. Chase has our next assignment. Here's your chewy."

"Okay, guys," Mr. Chase said, "you did a great job getting the facts on what was happening on the boat. You know what happened, but we want to be sure our readers understand who the characters are. Let's take a close-up look at the people in the story."

Ask God for His help, and then turn to page 123. Read Jonah 1:10-17. Get a profile on each person by making a list in your notebook. Start by looking at each verse where you marked LORD and write out what you learned about God next to the correct reference on the notebook page.

---

who made the sea and the dry land."

41 10 Then the men became extremely frightened and they said to him, "How could you do this?" For the men knew that he was fleeing from the presence of the LORD, because he had told them.

123

Observation Worksheets

124

11 So **they** said to **him**, "What should **we** do to **you** that the sea may become calm for **us**?"—for the sea was becoming increasingly stormy.

12 **He** said to **them**, "Pick **me** up and throw **me** into the sea. Then the sea will become calm for **you**, for I know that on account of **me** this great storm has come upon **you**."

13 However, the **men** rowed desperately to return to land but **they** could not, for the sea was becoming even stormier against **them**.

14 Then **they** called on the LORD and said, "We earnestly pray, O LORD, do not let **us** perish on account of this **man's** life and do not put innocent blood on **us**; for **You**, O LORD, have done as **You** have pleased."

15 So **they** picked up Jonah, threw **him** into the sea, and the sea stopped its raging.

16 Then the **men** feared the LORD greatly, and **they** offered a sacrifice to the LORD and made vows.

17 And the LORD appointed a great fish to swallow **Jonah**, and **Jonah** was in the stomach of the fish three days and three nights.

Chapter 2

(page 39)

What I Learned About God

Jonah 1:14

He does as He pleases.

Jonah 1:17

He appointed a great fish to swallow Jonah.

What did you see about the LORD? The LORD does as He pleases. Do you remember last week's memory verses? Think about what you learned about the LORD in Psalm 135:5-6.

Psalm 135:6 WHERE does the Lord do as He pleases?

In heaven, in earth, in the seas, and in all the deeps

---

42 Write what you learn about God on the notebook page.

What I Learned About God

Jonah 1:14 **He does as He pleases.**

Jonah 1:17 **He appointed a great fish to swallow Jonah.**

Use the memory verse from Psalm 135:5–6 to answer the next question.

Psalm 135:6 WHERE does the Lord do as He pleases? **In heaven, in earth, in the seas, and in all the deeps**

Guided Instruction

Read the selected verses to list what you learned about Jonah.

43 What I Learned About Jonah

Jonah 1:10 Jonah was fleeing from God.

Jonah 1:12 Jonah admitted the storm was his fault.

Jonah 1:15 Jonah was thrown into the sea.

Jonah 1:17 Jonah spent three days and three nights in the stomach of the fish.

God does exactly as He pleases in heaven, in earth, in the seas, and in all deeps. God is God, and He doesn't answer to anyone else. He is sovereign. That means there is nothing in the universe that God does not have total, absolute, and complete control over. He is the ruler of the universe. God does exactly what He wants to do.

What else did you see? The LORD appointed a great fish to swallow Jonah. This shows us that God is our provider. He provided a fish to rescue Jonah. It also shows us how much God loves Jonah. Even though Jonah is going the wrong way, God sends a fish and saves Jonah's life.

Let's make a list about Jonah by looking at every place where you colored his name orange. Write out what you learn about Jonah from these references.

43

What I Learned About Jonah

Jonah 1:10

Jonah was fleeing from God.

Jonah 1:12

Jonah admitted the storm was his fault.

Jonah 1:15

Jonah was thrown into the sea.

Jonah 1:17

Jonah spent three days and three nights in the stomach of the fish.

WHAT do we learn about Jonah from this list? Jonah admits to the sailors he is running away from God. Jonah knows he is doing the wrong thing. Jonah also knows the storm is his fault. The storm is from God.

Now let's see what we can learn about the sailors. Look at everyplace you marked for these men and list what you learn about them in your notebook.

What I Learned About the Sailors

Jonah 1:10

They were extremely frightened.

Jonah 1:11

They asked what they should do to Jonah so the sea would become calm.

Jonah 1:13

They rowed desperately to return to land but could not.

Jonah 1:14

They called on the Lord. They prayed earnestly.

Jonah 1:15

They threw Jonah into the sea.

Jonah 1:16

They feared the Lord and offered a sacrifice to the Lord and made vows.

Guided Instruction

Read the select verses to list what you learned about the sailors.

 What I Learned About the Sailors

Jonah 1:10 They were extremely frightened.

Jonah 1:11 They asked what they should do to Jonah so the sea would become calm.

Jonah 1:13 They rowed desperately to return to land but could not.

Jonah 1:14 They called on the Lord. They prayed earnestly.

Jonah 1:15 They threw Jonah into the sea.

Jonah 1:16 They feared the Lord and offered a sacrifice to the Lord and made vows.

Guided Instruction

45 Read and discuss the text on page 42.

---

42   Week Two

45 Incredible! Did you notice that the sailors were extremely frightened when they found out that Jonah was running away from God? These sailors don't know the one true God (we saw in verse 5 that they called on their gods first), but they have witnessed the one true God's power and they fear Him. The word *fear* in Hebrew is *yare*, and it means "a reverence and awe." These sailors are in awe of God. They fear God more than Jonah does.

The sailors also try to return to the land instead of throwing Jonah overboard. And when that doesn't work, they call on God. They beg for mercy. They don't want God to punish them for throwing Jonah overboard. They think Jonah will die, and they don't want to get in trouble for shedding innocent blood.

The sailors recognize God does as He pleases. And look at how they offer a sacrifice to God and make vows after the storm stops. While these sailors may not have a relationship with God, you can see they respect and honor God as being God.

Isn't it surprising to see Jonah, who is God's prophet, rebelling and going away from God instead of following Him, while these men who don't know God fear, respect, and honor Him?

You have done a great job at getting the background on the main characters to write your next story. As you practice your new memory verses today, think about how these sailors called to God and God saved them from the storm. Pretty cool, huh?

(page 42)

46 

HONE THOSE SKILLS

"Wow, Max!" Molly said as she looked back at her notes. "I am so blown away at what we're learning about God! I'm amazed at His awesome power and that these sailors who didn't know God feared God and called on Him."

Man Overboard! 43

Max smiled. "We need to remember this the next time we get upset or worried. That way we will remember how powerful God is and go straight to Him for help! Let's do that right now. Let's talk to God."

All right, rookie reporter! Let's get started on today's assignment. As you have gathered the facts for your story, you marked a very important key word—*pray*—and its synonyms—*cried, call,* and *called*. Did you notice how important prayer is in your story? Let's review.

Look back at Jonah 1 on page 123.

(page 123)

OBSERVATION WORKSHEETS

JONAH

47 

Chapter 1

1 The word of the LoRD came to Jonah the son of Amittai saying,

2 "Arise, go to Nineveh the great city and cry against it, for their wickedness has come up before Me."

3 But Jonah rose up to flee to Tarshish from the presence of the LORD. So he went down to Joppa, found a ship which was going to Tarshish, paid the fare and went down into it to go with **them** to Tarshish from the presence of the LORD.

4 The LORD hurled a great wind on the sea and there was a great storm on the sea so that the ship was about to break up.

5 Then the **sailors** became afraid and every **man cried** to **his** god, and **they** threw the cargo which was in the ship into the sea to lighten it for **them.** But Jonah had gone below into the hold of the ship, lain down and fallen sound asleep.

6 S... ...are sleep-

Ask God to remind you of His availability at all times.

46 Turn to page 42 and read "Hone Those Skills."

47 Turn to page 123 and read the selected verses to answer the questions.

Guided Instruction

6 So the captain approached him and said, "How is it that you are sleeping? Get up, call on your god. Perhaps your god will be concerned about us so that we will not perish."

7 Each man said to his mate, "Come, let us cast lots so we may learn on whose account this calamity has struck us." So they cast lots and the lot fell on Jonah.

8 Then they said to him, "Tell us, now! On whose account has this calamity struck us? What is your occupation? And where do you come from? What is your country? From what people are you?"

9 He said to them, "I am a Hebrew, and I fear the Lord God of heaven who made the sea and the dry land."

10 Then the men became extremely frightened and they said to him, "How could you do this?" For the men knew that he was fleeing from the presence of the Lord, because he had told them.

123

124   *Observation Worksheets*

11 So they said to him, "What should we do to you that the sea may become calm for us?"—for the sea was becoming increasingly stormy.

12 He said to them, "Pick me up and throw me into the sea. Then the sea will become calm for you, for I know that on account of me this great storm has come upon you."

13 However, the men rowed desperately to return to land but they could not, for the sea was becoming even stormier against them.

14 Then they called on the Lord and said, "We earnestly pray, O Lord, do not let us perish on account of this man's life and do not put innocent blood on us; for You, O Lord, have done as You have pleased."

15 So they picked up Jonah, threw him into the sea, and the sea stopped its raging.

16 Then the men feared the Lord greatly, and they offered a sacrifice to the Lord and made vows.

17 And the Lord appointed a great fish to swallow Jonah, and Jonah was in the stomach of the fish three days and three nights.

Chapter 2

(page 43)

Jonah 1:5 WHO is praying to WHOM?

The sailors are praying to their gods.

WHAT happens? **Their gods don't answer so they throw the cargo overboard to lighten the ship.**

Did you notice that the word *god* is written with a little *g*? That's because this word *god* refers to false gods and not the one true God whose name is written with a capital *G*.

Jonah 1:6 WHAT does the captain tell Jonah to do?

Get up, call on your god so that they we will not perish.

WHY does the captain want Jonah to pray?

So they will not perish

Do we see Jonah praying? ____ Yes __**X**_ No

---

44   Week Two

Jonah 1:14 WHO prays to WHOM?

Sailors pray to the Lord.

WHAT did the sailors pray?

"O Lord, do not let us __**perish**__ on __**account**__ of this __**man's**__ __**life**__ and do not put __**innocent**__ __**blood**__ on us; for You, O Lord, have done as You have __**pleased**__."

Jonah 1:15 WHAT happens next?

They throw Jonah into the sea and the sea stops raging.

Jonah 1:16 HOW did the sailors respond to God stopping the storm?

They feared the Lord, offered a sacrifice to the Lord, and made vows.

Guided Instruction

Jonah 1:5 WHO is praying to WHOM?
The sailors are praying to their gods.

WHAT happens? Their gods don't answer so they throw the cargo overboard to lighten the ship.

Jonah 1:6 WHAT does the captain tell Jonah to do? Get up, call on your god so that they we will not perish.

Why does the captain want Jonah to pray? So they will not perish.

Do we see Jonah praying? __ Yes **X** No

Jonah 1:14 WHO prays to WHOM? Sailors pray to the Lord.

WHAT did the sailors pray? "O Lord, do not let us perish on account of this man's life and do not put innocent blood on us; for You, O Lord, have done as You have pleased."

Jonah 1:15 WHAT happens next? They throw Jonah into the sea and the sea stops raging.

Jonah 1:16 HOW did the sailors respond to God stopping the storm? They feared the Lord, offered a sacrifice to the Lord, and made vows.

Guided Instruction

48 Practice the memory verse by completing the verses on page 45.

"The <u>Lord</u> is <u>near</u> to <u>all</u> who <u>call</u> upon Him, to <u>all</u> who <u>call</u> upon Him in <u>truth</u>. He will <u>fulfill</u> the <u>desire</u> of those who <u>fear</u> Him; He will also <u>hear</u> their <u>cry</u> and will <u>save</u> them."

Psalm 145:18–19

(page 44)

Do you see how important prayer is? The sailors call on God and are saved. And after God answers, they thank Him by offering a sacrifice and making vows. Are you surprised to see that the sailors prayed instead of Jonah?

It also matters to WHOM you pray. When the sailors prayed to their gods, there was no answer because their gods are false gods. But when they called on the one true God, He heard and answered their prayers! What an amazing God we have!

Have you noticed as you practiced your memory verses this week that they are also about "calling on the Lord"?

Since reporters need good memory skills as well as a "nose for news," Mr. Chase wants you to write out this week's verses from memory. Look at the notebook and see if you can complete the verses without looking back at Day One on page 34. Let's see what you can do!

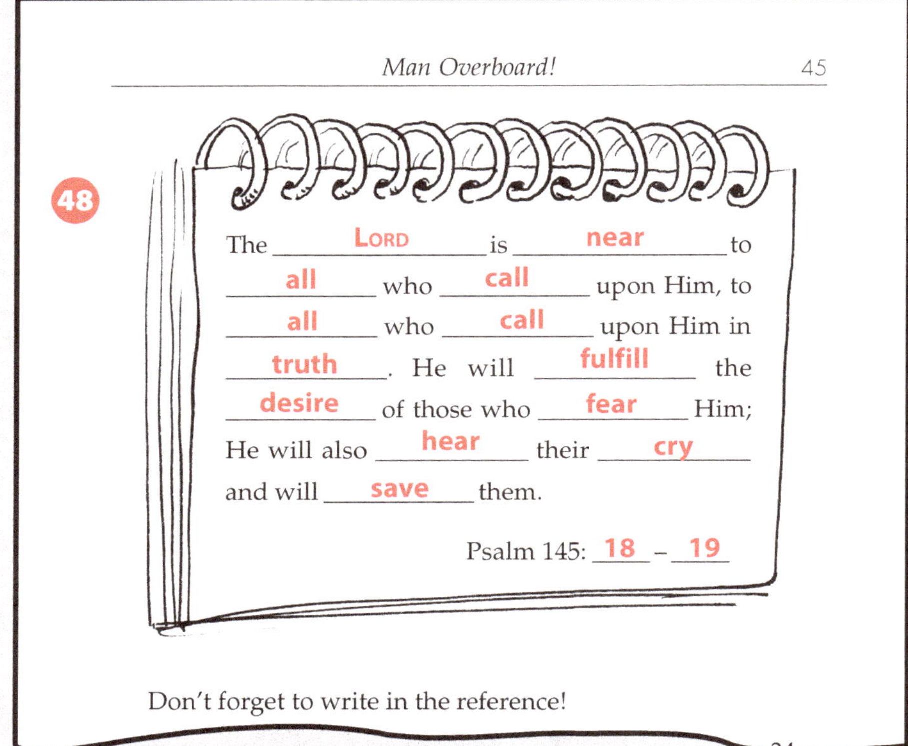

Don't forget to write in the reference!

(page 45)

So how did you do, rookie reporter? Look back on page 34 or at Psalm 145:18-19 in your Bible to make sure you got it right.

Have you cried to God and He helped you? Write what happened.

____

____

____

The next time something bad happens, you get into trouble, or you are afraid or upset, remember these verses. Remember, the Lord is near to all people who call upon Him. Run straight to Him! If you fear Him—if you honor and respect Him—God will hear your cry and save you!

You have done an outstanding job. You know just how important prayer is.

Guided Instruction

49 Lead a discussion and have students answer independently.

Guided Instruction

Ask God to impress you with the need to study His Word and obey His commands.

50 Turn to page 46 and read "Just the Right Shot!" and "A Whale of a Tale."

51 Reread Jonah 1:10–17 to complete the "Nineveh News" on page 49.

50

JUST THE RIGHT SHOT!

"Hey, Molly, come over here and look at what I found on the computer."

"What is it, Max?" Molly asked as she walked over to him.

"This is so cool. I've been researching what kind of fish might have swallowed Jonah for our story. Look at what I found."

Take a look, rookie reporter, at what Max discovered about the great fish in the book of Jonah.

A Whale of a Tale

There are many speculations about the kind of fish that swallowed Jonah, but no one knows for sure what kind it was. Some people think it was a great white shark. A 19-foot shark can swallow an adult person.

Large sperm whales have also been known to visit the Mediterranean Sea, where Jonah was caught in the storm. Sperm whales grow up to 70 feet long, so they have plenty of room for a man inside. In 1955 a sperm whale was killed and it had eaten a 405-pound squid. A sperm whale's esophagus is around 20 inches wide. And a whale doesn't chew its food, so Jonah could have been swallowed whole!

Or it could have just been a big fish. All we know for sure is that God provided this fish to rescue Jonah.

"Wow! Max, that so cool! So no one but God really knows what the great fish looked like. It could have been a whale, a shark, or just a great big fish."

"But we know one thing for sure: It happened to Jonah," Max said. "Jesus talks about Jonah being swallowed by a great fish.

"In Matthew 12:39-41, Jesus compares Jonah being inside the belly of the sea monster three days and three nights to His being in the tomb for three days and three nights," Max continued. "We know if Jesus says Jonah was inside the belly of a fish for three days and three nights, it happened just like He said!"

(page 47)

"That's right!" Molly said excitedly. "Jesus can't lie. He's the truth; He's God's Son. Even though some people may not believe that a great fish swallowed Jonah, we know it's true because Jesus said it."

"Mr. Chase said we'll need to draw the fish for our newspaper story," Max said.

"So what are you going to make your fish look like?" Molly asked.

Max grinned. "Just wait until you see it. It's going to be *awesome!* Mr. Chase will pick my drawing to go in the paper for sure!"

"We'll just see about that!" Molly countered.

WRITING THE STORY

Okay, rookie reporter, call on God before you get to work. Then grab your book and read Jonah 1:10-17.

Let's get started on your news story. Start by writing an

who made the sea and the dry land."

51 10 **Then** the **men** became extremely frightened and **they** said to him, "How could **you** do this?" For the **men** knew that **he** was fleeing from the presence of the LORD, because **he** had told **them**.

123

---

124   *Observation Worksheets*

11 So **they** said to **him**, "What should **we** do to **you** that the sea may become calm for **us**?"—for the sea was becoming increasingly stormy.

12 **He** said to **them**, "Pick **me** up and throw **me** into the sea. Then the sea will become calm for **you**, for I know that on account of **me** this great storm has come upon **you**."

13 However, the **men** rowed desperately to return to land but **they** could not, for the sea was becoming even stormier against **them**.

14 Then **they** called on the LORD and said, "We earnestly pray, O LORD, do not let **us** perish on account of this **man's** life and do not put innocent blood on **us**; for You, O LORD, have done as You have pleased."

15 So **they** picked up Jonah, threw **him** into the sea, and the sea stopped its raging.

16 Then the **men** feared the LORD greatly, and **they** offered a sacrifice to the LORD and made vows.

17 And the LORD appointed a great fish to swallow **Jonah**, and **Jonah** was in the stomach of the fish three days and three nights.

Chapter 2

Guided Instruction

52 Transfer the format of the "Nineveh News Issue 2" to large chart paper. As students reread Jonah 1:10–17 fill in the chart and have them complete page 49.

NINEVEH NEWS

ISSUE 2

BREAKING NEWS!

(headline) **Jonah Swallowed by Great Fish**

WEATHER:

Stormy (draw a picture)

As the storm continues to rage, Jonah tells the sailors he is fleeing from God. The sailors become extremely **frightened**. Jonah tells them to pick him up and **throw** him into the sea.

Instead the sailors desperately try to **row** to land, but the storm keeps them from shore. The sailors call on the **Lord** and plead with Him not to let them perish on account of Jonah. They pick up Jonah and throw him into the sea. Immediately the sea stops raging. The sailors offer a **sacrifice** and make vows to God.

What happens next is unbelievable! The Lord **appointed** a great **fish** to **swallow** Jonah. Jonah was in the stomach of the fish **three** days and **three** nights.

(page 47)

Let's get started on your news story. Start by writing an attention-getting headline using a few words for the top of the newspaper on page 49.

WHAT is the weather like? Draw a picture in the weather corner that shows what the weather is like, according to Jonah 1:10-17.

Fantastic! Now complete your news story by filling in the blanks.

Don't forget that Mr. Chase needs just the right picture for this

---

Man Overboard!   49

52

NINEVEH NEWS

ISSUE 2

**STORMY
(draw a picture)**

Weather

BREAKING NEWS!

Jonah Swallowed by Great Fish

(Put your headline here)

As the storm continues to rage, Jonah tells the sailors he is fleeing from God. The sailors become extremely **frightened**.
WHAT (verse 10)
Jonah tells them to pick him up and **throw** him into the sea.
WHAT (verse 12)

Instead the sailors desperately try to **row** to land, but the
WHAT (verse 13)
storm keeps them from shore. The sailors call on the **LORD**
WHO (verse 14)
and plead with Him not to let them perish on account of Jonah. They pick up Jonah and throw him into the sea. Immediately the sea stops raging. The sailors offer a **sacrifice** and make
WHAT (verse 16)
vows to God.

What happens next is unbelievable! The LORD **appointed** a great
WHAT (verse 17)
fish to **swallow** Jonah.
WHAT (verse 17)   WHAT (verse 17)
Jonah was in the stomach of the fish **three** days and
WHAT (verse 17)
three nights.
WHAT (verse 17)

<table>
<tr><td>

50   WEEK TWO

53

"EXTRA! EXTRA!"

Let's pretend we're on the ship and continue to act out Jonah's story. Flap that tablecloth faster and harder. The storm is increasing. Make more wind sounds and throw some water on those sailors as they desperately try to row to shore. Get on your knees and cry out to God. Pick up Jonah…and there he goes—splash! Here comes the great fish! Swish…Gulp! There goes Jonah!

How can you show Jonah in the great fish? One way is to move all the chairs from around the dining room or kitchen table and throw a large sheet over the table to cover it. Get under the table and pretend you are inside the great fish. Or you can get inside a big box. Or you can make your own great fish like Max and Molly did. Look at how they did it.

Materials Needed

- a king-sized sheet (Max and Molly used a black sheet)
- batting or material to stuff the fish's tail
- large pieces of white and black felt for the fish's eyes
- white and black thread or fabric glue
- scissors
- a 6′ x 5′ sport dome tent
- Velcro or safety pins to fasten the fish cover to the tent.

Instructions

Set up your dome tent following the tent instructions. Drape the king-sized sheet over the tent. The top of the sheet should stop just above the opening of the tent so that the doorway stays open. To secure the sheet in place on the tent, you need someone who sews to mark the sheet where it hits the tent poles. Then make two buttonholes on each side of the tent. Take a piece of Velcro and slide it through the buttonhole to secure the sheet to

</td></tr>
</table>

Guided Instruction

53 Turn to page 50 and read "Extra! Extra!"

Collect the materials and follow the instructions to make the "great fish" and continue to act out the events.

Use the Weekly Test to check memory and understanding.

Good job! God sees your progress and is pleased.

If you are a classroom teacher you may want to give your students a quiz on their memory verse. There is also a quiz on Week Two on page 139 to check the memory and understanding.

If you are a Sunday School teacher this is a great time to review the whole week by playing a game like the *Drawing Game* (See page 146 in the Teacher's Guide for instructions.)

Guided Instruction

the tent. Or instead of making buttonholes you can use safety pins and pin the sheet around the opening of the tent.

Next hold the white piece of felt up to one side of the tent and decide how big the eyes need to be. These will be the whites of the fish's eyes (look at the drawing). Draw two ovals on the felt and cut them out.

Now you need to cut out two black circles for the centers of the fish's eyes. Glue or sew the black circles onto the white ovals. Then pin or glue the eyes on each side of the sheet. Or you can sew the eyes on in the next step.

Now look at the sheet at the back of your tent. Take your scissors and cut off any excess so that the sheet still covers the tent all the way to the ground or floor. Take this extra material and draw two fish tails on it. Cut out the pieces and sew them together. Don't forget to leave an opening so you can stuff the tail. Stuff the tail with the batting and pin it to the sheet.

Unfasten the sheet and take it off the tent. Sew or glue on the eyes and tail. Then put your fish (the sheet) back over the tent and Velcro or safety pin it on. You have just created your own great fish!

3

JONAH 2

What an incredible week! Look at all we have discovered about Jonah and God. God has given Jonah a message to deliver, but God's prophet chooses to go the wrong way and do what he wants to do. God stops this wrong-way prophet in his tracks by sending a great storm and allowing Jonah to be thrown overboard and swallowed by a great fish.

Can you believe that a fish swallowed Jonah? Do you wonder what it's like inside the fish? WHAT will Jonah do? Will he get out alive? And WHY would God put Jonah inside the stomach of a fish? Let's find out.

MORE RESEARCH

54 "Hey, Molly, look over there. Are those ink marks on the floor?" asked Max.

52

WEEK 3

God is serious about His commands. Ask Him to keep you in His care and help you obey Him.

54 Turn to page 52 and read "Jonah 2" and "More Research."

Guided Instruction

"Yes, I think it's ink, but those don't look like marks. They look like…" Molly looked at Max horrified as he finished her sentence: "…dog paw prints. *SAM!*"

Molly started giggling as Max took off looking for you know who. Max and Molly ran into Mr. Chase out in the hallway. "Hey, Max, slow down. Are you looking for Sam? Don't worry, we found him. While you and Molly were at the printer, Miss Kate left some ink out and Sam got into it. When she tried to clean his paws, he took off and led the whole art department on quite a chase through the offices."

"Sam!" Max exclaimed while walking into the art department. "Why did you make such a mess?"

"It's my fault, Max," admitted Miss Kate. "I was playing with Sam and forgot I had the ink out. When we finished playing and I went back to work, Sam started sniffing out clues. He found the ink. But he's all cleaned up now and tired from his adventure. Why don't you and Molly do your research in here where you

Guided Instruction

55 Add new key words to bookmark. Turn to page 124 and read Jonah 2 aloud as students follow along. Have your students call each key word out loud as you read it, then mark it together, you on your transparency and they in their books. Allow time for them to mark their key words as they call it out.

God (Lord) (draw a purple triangle and color it yellow)

Jonah (color it orange)

Prayed (called, cried, prayer) (draw a purple bowl and color it pink)

Holy temple (color it blue)

WHERE (double underline in green words that denote place)

WHEN (draw a green clock over words that denote time)

---

54   WEEK THREE

can keep an eye on him. You can use some of our cool pens and pencils too."

"That sounds like a great idea," agreed Max

Okay, rookie reporter, grab your colored pencils. While Sam is napping we need to investigate Jonah 2 to find out what is happening now that Jonah is *inside* the great fish. Don't forget to talk to God first.

Turn to page 124. Read Jonah 2 and mark these key words and any synonyms for these words on your Observation Worksheets. Add any new key words to your key-word bookmark.

God (LORD) (draw a purple triangle and color it yellow)

Jonah (color it orange)

prayed (called, cried, prayer) (draw a purple and color it pink)

holy temple (color it blue)

Don't forget to mark the pronouns! And mark anything that tells you WHERE by double-underlining the WHERE in green. Mark anything that tells you WHEN by drawing a green clock  or a green circle like this ◯ .

Great work! Now let's figure out this week's memory verse.

(page 124)

Chapter 2

55 1 Then Jonah prayed to the LORD his God from the stomach of the fish,

2 And he said,

"I called out of my distress to the LORD,

And He answered me.

I cried for help from the depth of Sheol;

You heard my voice.

3 "For You had cast me into the deep,

Into the heart of the seas,

And the current engulfed me.

All Your breakers and billows passed over me.

4 "So I said, 'I have been expelled from Your sight.

Nevertheless I will look again toward Your holy temple.'

Guided Instruction

Observation Worksheets—Jonah 125

5 "Water encompassed me to the point of death.
The great deep engulfed me,
Weeds were wrapped around my head.

6 "I descended to the roots of the mountains.
The earth with its bars was around me forever,
But You have brought up my life from the pit, O LORD my God.

7 "While I was fainting away,
I remembered the LORD,
And my prayer came to You,
Into Your holy temple.

8 "Those who regard vain idols
Forsake their faithfulness,

9 But I will sacrifice to You,
With the voice of thanksgiving.
That which I have vowed I will pay.
Salvation is from the LORD."

10 Then the LORD commanded the fish, and it vomited Jonah up onto the dry land.

Chapter 3

(page 54)

Great work! Now let's figure out this week's memory verse. Take a look at the maze the staff artist has created for your newspaper article on Jonah being inside a great fish. Find the correct path through the great fish to discover this week's verse. Then fill in the blanks with the words in the correct order from the maze. Now look in Jonah 2 and find the reference. Practice saying this verse out loud three times in row, three times every day this week!

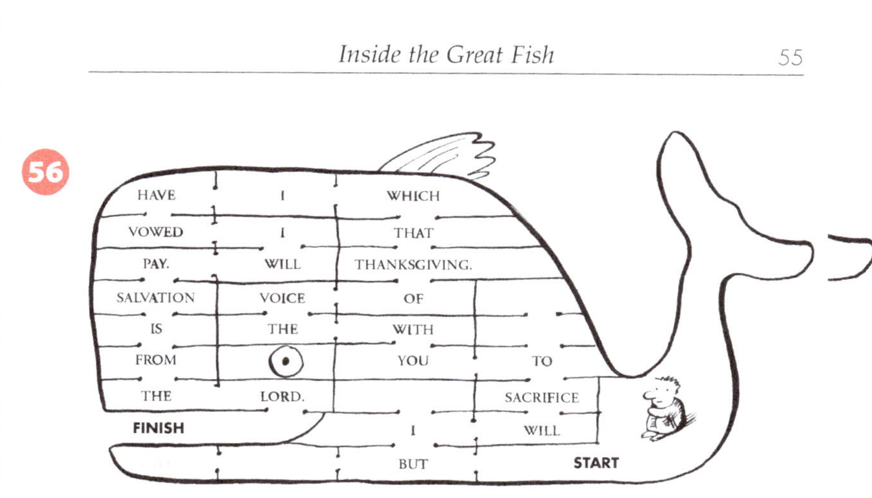

But **I** **will** **sacrifice** **to** **you** ,
with **the** **voice** **of** **thanksgiving** .
That **which** **I** **have** **vowed** **I**
will **pay** . **Salvation** **is** **from**
the **Lord** .

Jonah 2: **9**

All right! WHO is speaking to WHOM in this verse?
______**Jonah**______ is talking to ______**God**______.

Do you know what this is? Jonah is p **r a y i n g** !

Okay! We'll see you back in the newsroom to find out more details!

Guided Instruction

56 Find the correct path in the maze on page 55 to determine the memory verse.

"But I will sacrifice to you, with the voice of thanksgiving. That which I have vowed I will pay. Salvation is from the Lord."

Jonah 2:9

Copy the verse to an index card and practice saying it three times, three times a day.

WHO is speaking to WHOM in this verse? Jonah is talking to God.

Do you know what this is? Jonah is praying!

Guided Instruction

Ask God to guide you as you study His Word.

57 Turn to page 56 and read "Gather the Facts."

58 Read the selected verses in Jonah 2 to answer the questions.

57

GATHER THE FACTS

It's great to have you back at the news desk. You did a great job with your research yesterday. Now that we have our key words marked, we need to get the facts of what is happening inside the great fish. Don't forget to ask God for His help.

Turn to page 124. Read Jonah 2. Gather the facts for a big scoop. Be a good reporter and ask those 5 W's and an H.

Jonah 2:1 WHAT is Jonah doing?

(page 124)

Chapter 2

58 1 Then Jonah prayed to the LORD his God from the stomach of the fish,

2 And he said,
"I called out of my distress to the LORD,
And He answered me.
I cried for help from the depth of Sheol;
You heard my voice.

3 "For You had cast me into the deep,
Into the heart of the seas,
And the current engulfed me.
All Your breakers and billows passed over me.

4 "So I said, 'I have been expelled from Your sight.
Nevertheless I will look again toward Your holy temple.'

---

5 "Water encompassed me to the point of death.
The great deep engulfed me,
Weeds were wrapped around my head.

6 "I descended to the roots of the mountains.
The earth with its bars was around me forever,
But You have brought up my life from the pit, O LORD my God.

7 "While I was fainting away,
I remembered the LORD,
And my prayer came to You,
Into Your holy temple.

8 "Those who regard vain idols

(page 125)

8 "Those who regard vain idols
   Forsake their faithfulness,
9 But I will sacrifice to You,
   With the voice of thanksgiving.
   That which I have vowed I will pay.
   Salvation is from the LORD."
10 Then the LORD commanded the fish, and it vomited Jonah up onto the dry land.

Chapter 3

(page 56)

Jonah 2:1 WHAT is Jonah doing?

Praying

WHY do you think Jonah is doing this?

He is distressed.

WHERE is Jonah?

In the stomach of the great fish

The WHERE question you just answered gives us a chance to talk about a very important investigative tool called *context*. When you study the Bible, it is very important to understand what is happening in the passage.

Context is a combination of two words: *con*, which means "with," and *text*, which means "what is written." Context is the setting in which something is found. When you check the context for a Bible passage, you look at the verses surrounding what you are studying. You also think about where the passage fits in the big picture of the chapter in that book of the Bible, and then how the book fits into the whole Bible. Context also includes:

- The place something happens. This is geographical context.

Guided Instruction

Jonah 2:1 WHAT is Jonah doing?
Praying

WHY do you think Jonah is doing this?
He is distressed.

WHERE is Jonah? **In the stomach of the great fish**

Guided Instruction

59 Read and discuss the questions on page 57.

Jonah 2:2 WHAT do we see about Jonah? HOW is he calling out to the LORD? "I called out of my <u>distress</u>."

WHAT is Jonah crying for? For <u>help</u> from the depth of <u>Sheol.</u>

60 Read and discuss the next two questions. Do you think Jonah thinks he's going to die? Does God want Jonah to die? Give reasons for both of your answers.

Jonah 1:17 WHAT did God do in Jonah 1:17? <u>He appointed a fish to swallow Jonah.</u>

Inside the Great Fish   57

Ask, WHERE is this happening? Is this taking place in Israel or the United States? WHERE is Jonah?

- The time in history an event happens. This is historical context. Ask, WHEN is this happening? Is it before Jesus came to die on the cross or after? WHEN does the story of Jonah happen?
- The customs of a group of people. This is cultural context. Ask, WHAT did people in Bible times wear? Did they wear tunics or shorts and T-shirts? WHAT or WHO did the people worship in Jonah's day?

Sometimes you can discover all these things from just the verses you're studying. Sometimes you have to study other passages of Scripture to find out more details. It's always important to be on the lookout for context because it helps you discover what the Bible is saying.

We know the context of Jonah 2 (WHERE Jonah is), so now let's find out WHY he is praying to God.

59 Jonah 2:2 WHAT do we see about Jonah? HOW is he calling out to the LORD?

"I called out of my _____**distress**_____."

WHAT is Jonah crying for?

For _____**help**_____ from the depth of _____**Sheol**_____

60 Do you know what *Sheol* is? In the Old Testament, *Sheol* is sometimes translated as "Hades," "the grave," or "the pit." It is the world of the dead.

Does Jonah think he is going to die? _**X**__ Yes _____ No

Does God want Jonah to die? _____ Yes _**X**__ No

HOW do you know? WHAT did God do in Jonah 1:17?

He appointed a fish to swallow Jonah.

58 WEEK THREE

We know God didn't want Jonah to die because He sent a great fish to keep Jonah from drowning.

Draw a picture for the newspaper readers. Show Jonah calling out to God in distress while inside the stomach of the great fish.

Cool artwork! Jonah is alive inside the fish. The fish swallowed Jonah, but he didn't chew him up. Jonah is awake and knows what is happening.

How would you feel if you were inside the belly of a fish? Would you be afraid and in distress like Jonah? Would you call out to God for help? Write HOW you would feel and WHAT you would do if God put you inside a great fish.

____

____

____

____

That would be scary, wouldn't it? Tomorrow we will find out more about what happened to Jonah. Don't forget to practice your memory verse (Jonah 2:9).

61 On page 58 draw a picture showing Jonah calling out to God.

62 Respond independently below the picture. HOW would you feel and WHAT would you do if God put *you* inside a great fish?

Practice saying the memory verse with a friend.

Guided Instruction

DAY THREE

God responds to your prayers. Ask Him to lead you to obey Him completely.

63 Turn to page 59 and read "Profile the Characters."

64 Turn to page 124 and reread Jonah 2 to complete the notes.

DAY THREE

63

PROFILE THE CHARACTERS

"Hey, Max!" Molly called out. "How do you like my drawing of Jonah praying to God inside the fish?"

"That's pretty cool. I like it! Now we need to get the facts on what God does next. Let's pray and head back to Jonah 2. We need to get more info for the next edition of the *Nineveh News.*"

All right, rookie reporter, now that you have talked to God, let's find out how God responds to Jonah's prayer. Turn to page 124 and read Jonah 2.

Let's find out WHAT God does by making a list in our notebooks.

(page 124)

Chapter 2

64 1 Then Jonah prayed to the LORD his God from the stomach of the fish,

2 And he said,
"I called out of my distress to the LORD,
And He answered me.
I cried for help from the depth of Sheol;
You heard my voice.
3 "For You had cast me into the deep,
Into the heart of the seas,
And the current engulfed me.
All Your breakers and billows passed over me.
4 "So I said, 'I have been expelled from Your sight.
Nevertheless I will look again toward Your holy temple.'

---

5 "Water encompassed me to the point of death.
The great deep engulfed me,
Weeds were wrapped around my head.
6 "I descended to the roots of the mountains.
The earth with its bars was around me forever,
But You have brought up my life from the pit, O LORD my God.
7 "While I was fainting away,
I remembered the LORD,
And my prayer came to You,
Into Your holy temple.
8 "Those who regard vain idols

(page 125)

8 "Those who regard vain idols
   Forsake their faithfulness,
9 But I will sacrifice to You,
   With the voice of thanksgiving.
   That which I have vowed I will pay.
   Salvation is from the LORD."
10 Then the LORD commanded the fish, and it vomited Jonah up onto the dry land.

Chapter 3

(page 59)

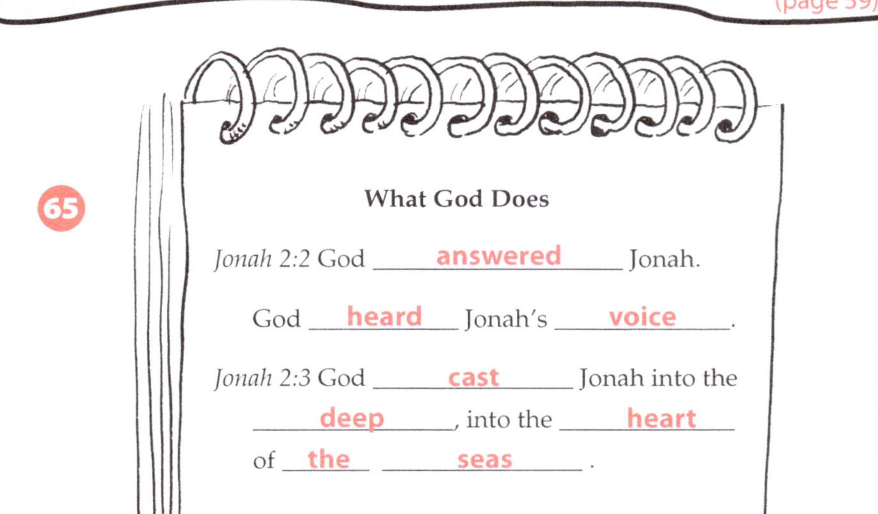

65

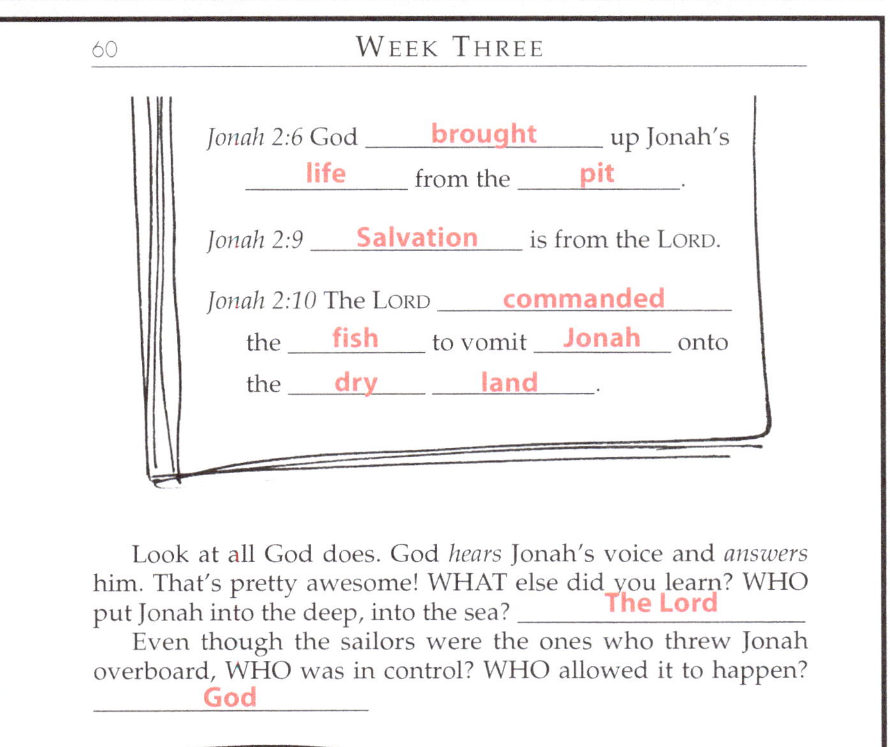

Look at all God does. God *hears* Jonah's voice and *answers* him. That's pretty awesome! WHAT else did you learn? WHO put Jonah into the deep, into the sea? ___The Lord___

Even though the sailors were the ones who threw Jonah overboard, WHO was in control? WHO allowed it to happen? ___God___

65 Read the selected verses to fill in the box "What God Does."

What God Does

Jonah 2:2 God <u>answered</u> Jonah. God <u>heard</u> Jonah's <u>voice</u>.

Jonah 2:3 God <u>cast</u> Jonah into the <u>deep</u>, into the <u>heart</u> of <u>the</u> <u>seas</u>.

Jonah 2:6 God <u>brought</u> up Jonah's <u>life</u> from the <u>pit</u>.

Jonah 2:9 <u>Salvation</u> is from the LORD.

Jonah 2:10 The Lord <u>commanded</u> the <u>fish</u> to vomit <u>Jonah</u> onto the <u>dry</u> <u>land</u>.

WHO put Jonah into the deep, into the sea? <u>The Lord</u>

WHO was in control? WHO allowed it to happen? <u>God</u>

Guided Instruction

Jonah 2:9 WHO saves Jonah? WHO saves us? God

Where does salvation come from? From the Lord

66 Fill in the list about Jonah on page 61.

Jonah

Jonah 2:4 Jonah has been expelled from God's sight.

Jonah 2:4 Jonah will look again to God's holy temple.

Jonah 2:5 Water encompassed Jonah to the point of death. The great deep engulfed Jonah. Weeds were wrapped around his head.

Jonah 2:6 Jonah descended to the roots of the mountains. The earth with its bars was around Jonah.

Jonah 2:7 Jonah was fainting away. Jonah remembered the LORD. And his prayer came to God in His holy temple.

Jonah 2:9 Jonah will sacrifice to the Lord with the voice of thanksgiving, what Jonah vowed he will pay.

Jonah 2:10 Jonah was vomited up by the fish onto dry land.

(page 60)

Look at Jonah 2:9. WHO saves Jonah? And WHO saves us? God saves us. This is called "salvation."

WHERE does salvation come from? __From the Lord__

Isn't that wonderful? God is the one who put Jonah into the sea, and God is the one who saves Jonah. WHO commanded the fish to vomit Jonah out? _______ That's right!

Once again you see that God is in control of everything. He made the fish vomit Jonah out. Wow! We bet that was pretty gross!

Now that you have seen just how awesome God is, take a closer look at WHAT happens to Jonah as he is cast into the sea. Fill in the list on Jonah in your notebook.

(page 61)

66

Jonah

Jonah 2:4 Jonah has been ___expelled___ from God's ___sight___.

Jonah 2:4 Jonah will ___look___ again to God's ___holy___ ___temple___.

Jonah 2:5 ___Water___ encompassed Jonah to the point of ___death___. The great ___deep___ ___engulfed___ Jonah. ___Weeds___ were wrapped around his ___head___.

Jonah 2:6 Jonah ___descended___ to the roots of the ___mountains___. The ___earth___ with its ___bars___ was around Jonah.

Jonah 2:7 Jonah was ___fainting___ away. Jonah ___remembered___ the Lord. And his ___prayer___ came to God in His ___holy___ ___temple___.

Jonah 2:9 Jonah will ___sacrifice___ to the Lord with the ___voice___ of ___thanksgiving___, what Jonah ___vowed___ he will ___pay___.

Jonah 2:10 Jonah was ___vomited___ up by the fish onto dry land.

Guided Instruction

Look up and read 2 Chronicles 6:24. WHAT are God's people to do when they sin against God? They are to <u>return</u> to God and <u>confess</u> God's name, and <u>pray</u> and make <u>supplication</u> before God in this <u>house</u>.

 **67** Draw a picture of what is happening to Jonah.

WHAT does Jonah do? Jonah 2:7 He <u>remembered</u> the Lord and p <u>r</u> <u>a</u> <u>y</u> s.

Practice saying the memory verse.

---

62   WEEK THREE

Unbelievable! Look at all that happens to Jonah. He is expelled from God's sight, but Jonah says, "I will look again toward Your holy temple" (verse 4). WHAT does that mean?

Look up and read 2 Chronicles 6:24.

2 Chronicles 6:24 WHAT are God's people to do when they sin against God?

They are to ____**return**____ to God and ____**confess**____ God's name, and __**pray**__ and make __**supplication**__ before God in this ____**house**____.

Jonah knows he has sinned. But he also knows what to do about his sin. Jonah knows he is to return to God. So that's what Jonah is doing when he says he will look again toward God's holy temple. Jonah is looking to God.

Now look at your list and notice what Jonah experiences in verses 5-7 as he is cast into the deep. Draw a picture in the box to show your readers what is happening to Jonah.

67

Terrific! Can you imagine what it would feel like to have the breakers and billows (waves and surges of waters) pass over you as seaweed wraps around your head?

Inside the Great Fish   63

As Jonah descends into the deep, fainting away, WHAT does he do? Look at Jonah 2:7.

He ____**remembered**____ the LORD and p __**r**__ __**a**__ __**y**__ __**s**__.

Great work! Tomorrow you will take a closer look at Jonah's prayer. Don't forget to practice your memory verse!

Guided Instruction

DAY FOUR

Pray for God's guidance during this study.

68 Turn to page 63 and read "The Scoop on Jonah's Prayer."

69 Reread Jonah 2 to answer the questions.

(page 63)

DAY FOUR

68

THE SCOOP ON JONAH'S PRAYER

"Hey, kids, how's it going?" Mr. Chase asked as he walked into the newsroom.

"We're doing great," Max replied. "We have uncovered some great info on God as Jonah prayed to Him inside the fish."

"And," Molly added, "we discovered what it was like for Jonah as he was thrown into the deep, the waves crashing over his head as he sank deeper and deeper into the sea. Take a look at our pictures."

"Those are some great shots. You two are turning into quite the reporters. Now that you have gathered the facts about Jonah and God, are you ready to take a closer look at Jonah's prayer?"

"We're ready!" Molly and Max exclaimed.

How about you, rookie reporter? Ask God for His help, and then head back to Jonah 2.

Turn to page 124 and read Jonah 2.

(page 124)

69 Chapter 2

1 Then Jonah prayed to the LORD his God from the <u>stomach</u> of the fish,

2 And he said,

"I called out of my distress to the LORD,

And He answered me.

I cried for help from the depth of <u>Sheol</u>;

You heard my voice.

3 "For You had cast me into the <u>deep</u>,

Into the <u>heart of the seas</u>,

And the current engulfed me.

All Your breakers and billows passed over me.

4 "So I said, 'I have been expelled from Your sight.

Nevertheless I will look again toward Your holy temple.'

(page 125)

5 "Water encompassed me to the point of death.

The great deep engulfed me,

Weeds were wrapped around my head.

6 "I descended to the roots of the mountains.

The <u>earth</u> with <u>its</u> bars was around me forever,

But You have brought up my life from the pit, O LORD my God.

7 "While I was fainting away,

I remembered the LORD,

And my prayer came to You,

Into Your holy temple.

8 "Those who regard vain idols

(page 125)

8 "Those who regard vain idols
   Forsake their faithfulness,
9 But I will sacrifice to You,
   With the voice of thanksgiving.
   That which I have vowed I will pay.
   Salvation is from the LORD."
10 Then the LORD commanded the fish, and it vomited Jonah up onto the dry land.

Chapter 3

(page 63)

Scoop the competition by asking the 5 W's and an H.

Jonah 2:7 WHAT did Jonah do when he was fainting away?

He remembered the Lord and prayed.

64   WEEK THREE

WHERE did Jonah's prayer come to God?

To God's holy temple

Jonah has been going the wrong way, but now he is going the right way by looking to God in His holy temple.

Jonah 2:9 WHAT does Jonah say he will do?

Sacrifice to God

HOW is Jonah going to do that?

With the **voice** of **thanksgiving**

WHAT did Jonah realize?

Salvation is from the **Lord**.

(70) Wow! That's a pretty incredible prayer, isn't it? Jonah prays to God with thanksgiving. After trying to run away from God, now Jonah realizes he needs to turn back to God. God is the One who put him inside the fish, and only God can save him.

Sometime during the three days and three nights Jonah sits inside the great fish, he goes from crying out for help to turning to God with a "voice of thanksgiving."

WHY should Jonah be thankful?

____

... is inside the fish ... he disobeyed

Guided Instruction

Jonah 2:7 WHAT did Jonah do when he was fainting away? He remembered the Lord and prayed.

WHERE did Jonah's prayer come to God? To God's holy temple

Jonah 2:9 WHAT does Jonah say he will do? Sacrifice to God

HOW is Jonah going to do that? With the voice of thanksgiving

WHAT did Jonah realize? Salvation is from the Lord.

(70) Read and discuss the rest of the questions and have students answer independently.

Guided Instruction

71 Read "Merciful God" on page 65.

72 Respond independently to the application questions on pages 66-67.

(page 64)

How about you? Jonah is inside the fish because he disobeyed God. You may not be inside a great fish, but maybe something bad has happened. Maybe you're in a bad situation because you haven't done what is right. Maybe your parents have put you on restriction. You know you are in trouble. WHAT do you need to do?

____

Inside the Great Fish   65

List three things you can thank God for.

1. _______________________________________

2. _______________________________________

3. _______________________________________

Now do it! Thank God!

Think back a minute. In Jonah 1:2, WHAT did God tell Jonah to do?_______________________________________

Did Jonah obey? ____ Yes   ____ No

Did you know that when you disobey there are consequences for your actions? Look at the consequences of Jonah's actions. He was in a horrible storm and was thrown overboard. He was swallowed by a great fish. Pretty bad, but it could have been a lot worse. God could have let Jonah drown. Instead we see that God is merciful. Mercy means not giving someone the punishment he or she deserves. That's why Jonah is able to thank God. He knows that he sinned against God and deserves to die, but instead God gives him mercy!

Max has done a study on God. Take a look at Max's notes.

71

Merciful God

Because God is a holy God, He must punish sin. In Romans 3:23 God tells us that we are all sinners. We sin when we break God's commandments. When we disobey our moms or dads, that's sin. When we are mean to our brothers and sisters, and when we use hurtful words to them or our friends, that's sin. And when we don't tell

66 WEEK THREE

the truth, that's sin also. Sin is knowing the right thing to do but not doing it (James 4:17).

God punishes sin. But in His mercy for us, He had Jesus take the punishment for our sins instead of us.

When we agree with God that we are sinners and when we believe that Jesus is God's Son and that He died on a cross for our sins, we are ready to ask Him to be our Savior and Lord! And when we do that, God forgives us for our sins! Now that's a reason to be thankful!

As Jonah sits inside the great fish, he realizes that he has sinned and that only God can save him. That's why Jonah says, "Salvation is from the LORD" (Jonah 2:9). Did you know that only Jesus can save you from your sins? Have you asked Jesus to forgive you?

72 Can you think of a time in your life when you deserved to be punished but you received mercy from someone instead? Write out what happened and who showed you mercy.

____

____

____

Has there ever been a time when someone hurt you? ______

WHAT did you do? Did you try to hurt him or her back?

____

____

Guided Instruction

Jonah 2:10 WHAT happens after Jonah returns to God and prays? <u>God commands the fish and it vomits him up on dry land.</u>

Practice saying the memory verse with a friend.

If you want to follow God, you need to be merciful to other people just like God has been merciful to you. So the next time someone hurts you, try to be kind instead of being mean back.

God uses awful circumstances—a huge storm and a great fish—to get Jonah's attention. Jonah finally turns to God and prays. Has God ever had to do something drastic to get your attention so that you turned to Him for help? Write out what happened.

____

____

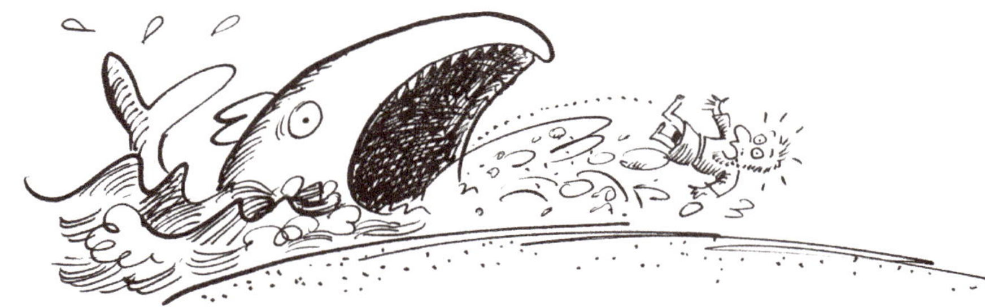

Jonah 2:10 WHAT happens after Jonah returns to God and prays?

God commands the fish and it vomits him up on dry land.

Wouldn't this make a great illustration for the newspaper? Jonah has turned from going the wrong way to going the right way—to God. Isn't that amazing? So God commands the fish to vomit Jonah onto land. Remember, God has a plan for Jonah.

Don't forget to practice your memory verse. This verse will remind you to give thanks to God. Salvation comes from Him.

(page 68)

WRITE THE STORY

Our research is done, and it's time to write the news story. Grab your book and your colored pencils. Don't forget to talk to God first. We need God to be our Master Editor so we can get this story just right.

Turn to page 124 and read Jonah 2.

All right! You have the facts. Write your headline in just a few

---

(page 124)

Chapter 2

1 Then Jonah prayed to the LORD his God from the stomach of the fish,

2 And he said,

"I called out of my distress to the LORD,

And He answered me.

I cried for help from the depth of Sheol;

You heard my voice.

3 "For You had cast me into the deep,

Into the heart of the seas,

And the current engulfed me.

All Your breakers and billows passed over me.

4 "So I said, 'I have been expelled from Your sight.

Nevertheless I will look again toward Your holy temple.'

Observation Worksheets—Jonah   125

5 "Water encompassed me to the point of death.

The great deep engulfed me,

Weeds were wrapped around my head.

6 "I descended to the roots of the mountains.

The earth with its bars was around me forever,

But You have brought up my life from the pit, O LORD my God.

7 "While I was fainting away,

I remembered the LORD,

And my prayer came to You,

Into Your holy temple.

8 "Those who regard vain idols

Ask God to help you report the story accurately.

73 Transfer the format of "Nineveh News: Issue 3" to large chart paper. As students reread Jonah 2 fill in the chart and have them complete page 69.

Guided Instruction

73

NINEVEH NEWS

ISSUE 3

BREAKING NEWS!

Big Fish Vomits Jonah on Dry Land!

WEATHER:

Calm (draw a picture)

Note: The sea has stopped its raging.

(page 125)

8   "Those who regard vain idols
    Forsake their faithfulness,
9   But I will sacrifice to You,
    With the voice of thanksgiving.
    That which I have vowed I will pay.
    Salvation is from the LORD."
10 Then the LORD commanded the fish, and it vomited Jonah up onto the <u>dry land.</u>

Chapter 3

(page 68)

All right! You have the facts. Write your headline in just a few words at the top of the newspaper on the next page.

WHAT is the weather like outside? Jonah 2 doesn't say since Jonah is inside the fish, but we do know from Jonah 1:15 that after Jonah was thrown into the sea, the storm stopped its raging. Draw a picture in the weather box of what you think the weather might be like now that the sea has stopped raging.

Now write the story by filling in the blanks on the front page of the *Nineveh News*. Great copy! Draw an illustration of the most amazing thing that happens in Jonah 2 so readers can see the action.

Inside the Great Fish   69

NINEVEH NEWS

ISSUE 3

BREAKING NEWS!

Calm
(draw a picture)
Weather

Big Fish Vomits Jonah on Dry Land!
(Put your headline here)

DRAW A PICTURE!

(page 69)

After Jonah gulps sea water and almost drowns, God sends a great **fish** to swallow Jonah. Inside the stomach of the fish, Jonah **prayed** to the LORD for **help** .

WHAT (Jonah 1:17)
WHAT (Jonah 2:1)
WHAT (Jonah 2:2)

In His great mercy and love, God **heard** Jonah's voice and **answered** him.

WHAT (verse 2)
WHAT (verse 2)

Jonah turns to God and goes from crying for help to sacrificing to God with a voice of **thanksgiving** . God's

WHAT (Jonah 2:9)

prophet realizes his s **i n** of disobedience and God's m **e r c y** in not letting him die.

After Jonah spends three days and three nights inside the fish, the LORD **commanded** the fish, and it **vomited** Jonah

WHAT (Jonah 2:10)
WHAT (Jonah 2:10)

up onto the **dry** **land** .

WHERE (Jonah 2:10)

In a surprising turn of events, God has saved this wrong-way prophet and turned him the right way!

---

70   WEEK THREE

LET'S PRINT IT!

74 What an exciting edition! This week we have seen just how far God will go to get our attention when we turn away from Him. And we've realized just how loving and merciful He is when we turn back to Him.

Jonah prayed with thanksgiving, and God wants us to come to Him in prayer too. God wants us to thank Him and depend on Him just like Jonah did when he prayed inside the fish.

Why don't you write out a prayer of thanksgiving to God? Thank Him for who He is and what He has done for you. Ask Him to help you with something specific. Write down your prayer.

75 ___________________________________

____

____

____

All right! Way to go! WHAT will happen now that the fish has vomited Jonah out? WHERE will Jonah go? Will he get on another ship? We'll find out next week.

Don't forget to say your memory verse out loud to a grown-up this week.

Guided Instruction

After Jonah gulps sea water and almost drowns, God sends a great **fish** to swal ow Jonah. Inside the stomach of the fish, Jonah **prayed** to the Lord for **help**. In His great mercy and love, God **heard** Jonah's voice and **answered** him.

Jonah turns to God and goes from crying for help to sacrificing to God with a voice of **thanksgiving**. God's prophet realizes his s **i n** of disobedience and God's m **e r c y** in not letting him die.

After Jonah spends three days and three nights inside the fish, the Lord **commanded** the fish, and it **vomited** Jonah up onto the **dry** **land**.

In a surprising turn of events, God has saved this wrong-way prophet and turned him the right way!

74 Turn to page 70 and read "Let's Print It!"

75 Write down your personal prayer.

Practice saying the memory verse to a grown-up.

Use the quiz on Week Three on page 140 to check memory and understanding

You may want to play a game like *The Matching Game* on page 147 or the *Drawing Game* on page 146 for the kids to review what they have learned.

Guided Instruction

76 Read "Extra! Extra!" and lead a discussion. Continue to act out the events in Jonah 2.

(page 70)

"EXTRA! EXTRA!"

76 Are you ready to continue acting out Jonah's story? Last week we left Jonah inside the great fish. So get back under the dining room table or inside the great fish you created.

Think about what it might have been like inside the fish. Was there any light inside or was it very dark? If you think it was dark, turn out the lights, or if you are inside the tent, zip it up.

WHAT did it smell like in the belly of the fish? Open a can of tuna fish or sardines. Smell them. And do you remember the seaweed that was wrapped around Jonah's head? Ask a grown-up to help you boil some green noodles to use as seaweed. (Or you can use regular noodles and add green food coloring to make

Inside the Great Fish   71

them green.) Let the noodles cool. Put this slimy, cold "spaghetti seaweed" around your head. Sit inside the fish again. WHAT did it feel like to be in the belly of the fish?

WHAT might Jonah eat the three days he is inside the fish? WHAT sounds might he hear? HOW do you think he would feel?

Remember, Jonah prayed, so say your memory verse out loud.

Use your imagination and what you have learned to act out this astonishing event!

4

A SECOND CHANCE

JONAH 3

Wow! Wasn't that awesome to get a close-up look at what it was like for Jonah when he was thrown into the deep and swallowed by a great fish? You saw firsthand the consequences of disobeying God and choosing to do what you want to do instead of what God wants you to do. And you saw just how loving, merciful, and amazing God is. Look at all He did to get Jonah's attention and to get him going the right way.

Are you ready to find out WHAT happens now that the fish has vomited Jonah onto shore? WHAT will Jonah do? Have the three days and three nights inside the fish changed Jonah's heart? Will he obey God and go to Nineveh? Let's find out.

DAY ONE

77

A NEW BEAT

"Hey, Molly!" Max called out. "Come over here. Look at Sam sitting at the computer. He thinks he's writing the next story for our paper."

72

DAY ONE

Ask God to bless your study of His powerful Word and help you apply it today.

77 Turn to page 72 and read Jonah 3 and "A New Beat."

Guided Instruction

78 Add new key words to bookmark. Turn to page 125 and read Jonah 3 aloud as students follow along and call out each key word as you mark them together as we noted on page 16.

God (LORD) (draw a purple triangle and color it yellow)

Jonah (color it orange)

Proclaim (proclamation, cried out, called) (circle it in blue and color it yellow)

Believed (draw a purple book and color it green)

WHERE (double-underline in green words that denote place)

WHEN (draw a green clock over words that denote time)

"Hey, Sam, old boy." Molly walked up and rubbed his head. "What have you discovered, hmmm? I'm not sure I can read those notes. Why don't you get down and sniff out some clues while Max and I head back to the book of Jonah. We need to find out what is happening now that Jonah is out of the great fish."

"I'll pray," Max volunteered as Sam jumped down and started sniffing around. "Then we can get started."

All right! Rookie reporter, it's time to head to Jonah 3. We need to grab our colored pencils and discover more of the story.

Turn to page 125. Read Jonah 3 and mark the following key words and any synonyms for these words on your Observation Worksheets. Add any new key words to your key-word bookmark.

God (LORD) (draw a purple triangle and color it yellow)

Jonah (color it orange)

proclaim (proclamation, cried out, called) (circle it in blue and color it yellow)

believed (draw a purple book and color it green)

Don't forget to mark the pronouns! And mark anything that tells you WHERE by double-underlining the WHERE in green. Mark anything that tells you WHEN by drawing a green clock or green circle: ⃝ .

Now gather the facts. Ask the 5 W's and an H questions.

(page 125)

Chapter 3

1 Now the word of the LORD came to Jonah the second time, saying,

2 "Arise, go to Nineveh the great city and proclaim to it the proclamation which I am going to tell you."

3 So Jonah arose and went to Nineveh according to the word of the LORD. Now Nineveh was an exceedingly great city, a three days' walk.

4 Then Jonah began to go through the city one day's walk; and he cried out and said, "Yet forty days and Nineveh will be overthrown."

5 Then the people of Nineveh believed in God; and they called a fast and put on sackcloth from the greatest to the least of them.

6 When the word reached the king of Nineveh, he arose from his throne, laid aside his robe from him, covered himself with sackcloth and sat on the ashes.

126 *Observation Worksheets*

7 He issued a proclamation and it said, "In Nineveh by the decree of the king and his nobles: Do not let man, beast, herd, or flock taste a thing. Do not let them eat or drink water.

8 "But both man and beast must be covered with sackcloth; and let men call on God earnestly that each may turn from his wicked way and from the violence which is in his hands.

9 "Who knows, God may turn and relent and withdraw His burning anger so that we will not perish."

10 When God saw their deeds, that they turned from their wicked way, then God relented concerning the calamity which He had declared He would bring upon them. And He did not do it.

Chapt

Guided Instruction

(79) Reread the selected verses to answer the questions.

Jonah 3:1 WHAT is happening? The word of the Lord came to Jonah a second time.

Jonah 3:2 WHAT did God tell Jonah to do? Arise, go to Nineveh and proclaim what God says.

Jonah 1:1–2 Has this happened before? Yes

Jonah 3:1 HOW many times has God asked Jonah to do this? Two times

Read and discuss the rest of the questions. Answer independently.

Jonah 3:3 What does Jonah do? He goes to Nineveh according to the word of the Lord.

---

(79) Jonah 3:1 WHAT is happening?
The word of the Lord came to Jonah a second time.

Jonah 3:2 WHAT did God tell Jonah to do?
Arise, go to Nineveh and proclaim what God says.

Look back at Jonah 1:1-2. Has this happened before?
Yes

Jonah 3:1 HOW many times has God asked Jonah to do this? __Two__ times

How about you? How long does it take you to obey? How many times do your parents ask you to do something before you do it?

____

Do you think it is "true" obedience if you don't do what you're told the first time you are asked? ____ Yes ____ No

WHY should you obey the first time?

____

Jonah 3:3 WHAT does Jonah do?
He goes to Nineveh according to the word of the Lord.

Do you think Jonah wanted to go to Nineveh this time? Or do you think Jonah felt like "his back was against a wall"? When someone says, "My back is against a wall," it means he or she is in a hard situation. Things are tough and hard to get around, so the person doesn't feel like he has a choice.

Did Jonah obey because of his circumstances (he didn't want to go through another storm and end up inside the belly of a fish again)? Or did Jonah obey because he had a change of heart?

WHY do you think Jonah goes to Nineveh?

____

WHAT would you do if God asked you to do something you didn't want to do?

____

WHY?____

Do you realize there are consequences if you disobey God?

_____ Yes   _____ No

Do you want God to put you in a hard situation like Jonah was in to get your attention? _________ Think about it. He will.

And if there is something you know God wants you to do, then go to God, and tell Him you want to obey, and you want Him to help you.

Isn't it awesome that God gives Jonah a second chance to obey Him? God has a plan for Jonah. And He isn't going to let him off the hook yet.

Guided Instruction

80 Use the code to unscramble the memory verse on page 76.

Let men call on God earnestly that each may turn from his wicked way and from the violence which is in his hands.

Jonah 3:8

Copy the memory verse to an index card and practice saying it three times a day for three days.

(page 77)

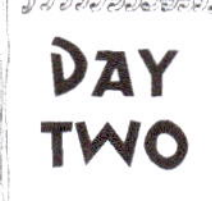

DAY TWO

SPREAD THE NEWS!

All right! Now that Jonah obeyed God and headed to Nineveh, we need to take another look at this city and find out what God's message is so we can spread the news.

Ask your Master Editor for His help, and then turn to page 125 and read Jonah 3:1-5.

Pull out your notebook. Gather the facts by making a list on Nineveh. Do you remember what you learned about Nineveh when God first told Jonah to go there? If you don't, read Jonah 1:2 again. Add these facts about Nineveh to your notebook too!

(page 125)

dry land.

Chapter 3

1 Now the word of the LORD came to Jonah the second time, saying,

2 "Arise, go to Nineveh the great city and proclaim to it the proclamation which I am going to tell you."

3 So Jonah arose and went to Nineveh according to the word of the LORD. Now Nineveh was an exceedingly great city, a three days' walk.

4 Then Jonah began to go through the city one day's walk; and he cried out and said, "Yet forty days and Nineveh will be overthrown."

5 Then the people of Nineveh believed in God; and they called a fast and put on sackcloth from the greatest to the least of them.

6 When the word reached the king of Nineveh, he arose from his throne,

(page 77)

Ask your Master Editor for His help, and then turn to page 125 and read Jonah 3:1-5.

Pull out your notebook. Gather the facts by making a list on Nineveh. Do you remember what you learned about Nineveh when God first told Jonah to go there? If you don't, read Jonah 1:2 again. Add these facts about Nineveh to your notebook too!

Facts on Nineveh

Jonah 1:2 Nineveh is a __**great**__ city filled with w __**i c k e d n e s s**__.

Jonah 3:2-3 Nineveh was an exceedingly __**great**__ city, a __**three**__ days' __**walk**__.

Jonah 3:4 Nineveh will be __**overthrown**__ in __**40**__ days.

Guided Instruction

DAY TWO

God wants you to understand how serious it is to follow His commands. Ask Him to give you a special message today.

81 Turn to page 77 and read "Spread the News!"

82 Read the selected verses to complete the notebook page.

Facts on Nineveh

Jonah 1:2 Nineveh is a great city filled with w i c k e d n e s s.

Jonah 3:2–3 Nineveh was an exceedingly great city, a three days' walk.

Jonah 3:4 Nineveh will be overthrown in 40 days.

Guided Instruction

Genesis 10:11–12 WHERE is Nineveh located? In A s s y r i a

HOW did the people in Nineveh and the children of Israel (the Jews) get along? Were they friends of enemies? Enemies for more than 100 years

WHAT were the Assyrians (the people in Nineveh) like? Fierce warriors

WHOM did they worship: the one true God or idols? Idols

83 Read and discuss the questions on page 78. Answer independently.

84 Turn to page 125 and read the selected verses to answer the questions.

Jonah 3:2 WHAT does God want Jonah to do in Nineveh? Proclaim what God says

---

78   WEEK FOUR

Do more investigative work by looking at a cross-reference. Pull out your Bible. Look up and read Genesis 10:11-12.

Genesis 10:11 WHERE is Nineveh located?

In A s s y r i a

 Turn back to your map on page 19 and take another look at where Nineveh is located. Today the ruins of Nineveh are in Iraq, on the east bank of the Tigris River, opposite the city of Mosul.

A good way to get more information on Nineveh is to look it up in a Bible dictionary. Since Max and Molly have already done some research on Nineveh, turn to page 18 and read again Max and Molly's notes to answer the next three questions.

HOW did the people in Nineveh and the children of Israel (the Jews) get along? Were they friends or enemies?

Enemies for more than 100 years

WHAT were the Assyrians (the people in Nineveh) like?

Fierce warriors

WHOM did they worship: the one true God or idols?

Idols

 Now turn to Jonah 3 on page 125.

Jonah 3:2 WHAT does God want Jonah to do in Nineveh?

Proclaim what God says

Do you know what it means to *proclaim?* It means "to call, cry out, or preach." God has a message He wants Jonah to tell the people in Nineveh.

Jonah 3:4 WHAT does Jonah cry out? WHAT is going to happen to Nineveh?

Nineveh will be overthrown.

WHEN is God going to do this?

In forty days

Remembering what you learned about Nineveh, WHY would God want to overthrow this city?

____

Jonah 3:5 HOW did the people of Nineveh respond to Jonah's proclamation?

They believed God.

WHAT two things did they do?

1. **Called a fast**

2. **Put on sackcloth**

Unbelievable! These enemies of Israel, who were wicked and cruel, listened to Jonah's message and believed in God. And they backed up what they believed with their actions. They called a fast—a time of not eating—and put on sackcloth—special clothes. We'll find out more about fasting and sackcloth tomorrow.

Don't forget to practice your memory verse!

Guided Instruction

Jonah 3:4 WHAT does Jonah cry out? WHAT is going to happen to Nineveh? **Nineveh will be overthrown.**

WHEN is God going to do this? **In forty days**

WHY would God want to overthrow this city? Discuss and answer independently.

Jonah 3:5 HOW did the people of Nineveh respond to Jonah's proclamation? **They believed God.**

WHAT two things did they do?

1. **Called a fast**

2. **Put on sackcloth**

Practice saying the memory verse.

Guided Instruction

DAY THREE

Ask God to open your mind and heart to study His Word.

85 Turn to page 80 and read "At the Scene."

86 Add new key words to bookmark. Turn to page 125 and reread Jonah 3:5–10 aloud as your students follow along and call out each key word as you mark them together as we noted on page 16.

King (color it blue)

Fast (circle it in brown)

Sackcloth (draw a black arch above the word)

Turn (turned) (draw a green arrow)

Relent (relented) (draw a red arrow and color the word yellow)

Anger (draw a black squiggly line through the word)

DAY THREE

AT THE SCENE

85 "Wow, Max," Molly said, "no wonder God wanted Jonah to go to Nineveh. He had a very important message for those people. In 40 days He was going to destroy their city."

"Yes, isn't it amazing that God loved those wicked people so much that He sent Jonah to warn them? Let's head back to Nineveh and find out what else happens. I'll pray and then we can get started."

Okay, rookie reporter, turn to page 125. Read Jonah 3:5-10 and mark the following key words on your Observation Worksheets. Add any new key words to your key-word bookmark.

king (color it blue)

fast (circle it in brown)

sackcloth (draw a black arch like this: ⌒)

turn (turned) (draw a green arrow)

relent (relented) (draw a red arrow and color the word yellow)

anger (draw a black squiggly line like this: ⋀⋁⋁)

All right! Let's get the scoop. Solve the crossword puzzle by asking the 5 W's and an H. Find out WHAT happens now that Jonah has preached God's message.

(page 125)

86

out and said, "Yet forty days and Nineveh will be overthrown."

5 **Then** the people of Nineveh believed in God; and they called a fast and put on sackcloth from the greatest to the least of them.

6 **When** the word reached the king of Nineveh, he arose from his throne, laid aside his robe from him, covered himself with sackcloth and sat on the ashes.

---

126 *Observation Worksheets*

7 **He** issued a proclamation and it said, "In Nineveh by the decree of the king and his nobles: Do not let man, beast, herd, or flock taste a thing. Do not let them eat or drink water.

8 "But both man and beast must be covered with sackcloth; and let men call on God earnestly that each may turn from his wicked way and from the violence which is in his hands.

9 "Who knows, God may turn and relent and withdraw His burning anger so that we will not perish."

10 When God saw their deeds, that they turned from their wicked way, then God relented concerning the calamity which He had declared He would bring upon them. And He did not do it.

Chapter 4

1 But it greatly displeased Jonah and he became angry.

A Second Chance 81

87

Guided Instruction

87 Read the selected verses to answer the questions and complete the crossword puzzle on page 81.

Guided Instruction

Jonah 3:5 WHAT did the people of Nineveh call for?

1. (across) A fast

Jonah 3:6 WHO did the word reach next?

2. (down) The king of Nineveh

Jonah 3:6 HOW did the king respond to the proclamation?

3. (across) He arose from his throne, laid aside his

4. (down) robe, covered himself with sackcloth and sat on

5. (across) the ashes.

Jonah 3:7 WHAT did the king issue?

6. (down) A proclamation

Jonah 3:7–8 WHAT was the proclamation? WHAT did the king tell the people to do? "Do not let man, beast, herd, or flock taste a thing. Do not let them

7. (down) eat or

8. (across) drink water.

9. (across) But both man and beast must be covered with sackcloth.

10. (across) Let men call on

11. (across) God earnestly that each may

12. (across) turn from his

13. (across) wicked way and from the

14. (across) violence which is in his hands."

(page 81)

Jonah 3:5 WHAT did the people of Nineveh call for?

1. (across) A ________fast________

Jonah 3:6 WHO did the word reach next?

2. (down) The _______king_______ of Nineveh

Jonah 3:6 HOW did the king respond to the proclamation?

3. (across) He arose from his ________throne________, laid aside his

---

82   WEEK FOUR

4. (down)________robe________, covered himself with sackcloth and sat on

5. (across) the ________ashes________.

Jonah 3:7 WHAT did the king issue?

6. (down) A ________proclamation________

Jonah 3:7-8 WHAT was the proclamation? WHAT did the king tell the people to do? "Do not let man, beast, herd, or flock taste a thing. Do not let them

7. (down) ________eat________ or

8. (across)________drink________ water.

9. (across) But both man and beast must be covered with ________sackcloth________.

10. (across) Let men ________call________ on

11. (across) ________God________ earnestly that each may

12. (across) ________turn________ from his

13. (across) ________wicked________ way and from the

14. (across) ________violence________ which is in his hands."

Jonah 3:9 WHAT is the king hoping God will do?

"God may turn and

15. (down)________relent________ and withdraw His burning

16. (down) ________anger________ so that we will not

17. (down) ________perish________ ."

Do you know what *sackcloth* is? Take a look at Max and Molly's research below.

Scratchy Coats

Sackcloth was a warm, dark material that was woven from goat or camel hair. Garments made of sackcloth felt rough and itchy against a person's skin.

Sackcloth was worn to show sorrow for sins. The harsh texture of the garment reminded people of how uncomfortable sin should be.

When people wore sackcloth and put ashes on their skin, they usually fasted as well. *Fasting* means they chose not to eat food or drink liquids.

Sackcloth, ashes, and fasting were outward expressions of hearts full of sorrow for wrong choices and sin.

What a scoop! Can you believe that these wicked people and their king not only hear Jonah's message, but they act on it? Everyone in Nineveh, including all the animals, wears itchy and uncomfortable clothes and goes without eating or drinking to show God they are sorry for their sins.

Jonah 3:9 WHAT is the king hoping God will do?

"God may turn and

15. (down) <u>relent</u> **and withdraw His burning**

16. (down) <u>anger</u> **so that we will not**

17. (down) <u>perish</u>**."**

88 Read the note "Scratchy Coats" on page 83.

Guided Instruction

89 Read and discuss the text on page 84. Have students answer independently.

90 Read 1 John 1:9 and answer the questions.

If we confess our sins, He is faithful and righteous to forgive us our sins and to cleanse us from all unrighteousness.

WHAT does the Bible tell us we should do when we sin? Confess our sin

WHAT will God do? Forgive our sins and cleanse us from all unrighteousness

91 Read and discuss the rest of the questions.

Practice saying the memory verse with a friend.

---

84   WEEK FOUR

89 How about you? Have you ever felt that kind of sorrow for your sins? Have you ever heard a message from your parents or your Sunday school teacher or as you did one of these Bible studies that made you realize you were sinning? WHAT did you do? Did you ignore it? Or did you feel sorry and ask God to forgive you? Also share what happened next.

____

____

____

90 Read 1 John 1:9:

If we confess our sins, He is faithful and righteous to forgive us our sins and to cleanse us from all unrighteousness.

WHAT does the Bible tell us we should do when we sin?

Confess our sin

WHAT will God do?

Forgive our sins and cleanse us from all unrighteousness

Isn't that amazing? If we confess our sins—that means we name our sins, we say what they are, and we are really sorry about what we have done wrong—God forgives us.

91 Nineveh was a sinful and wicked country. How about the country you live in? Does your country keep God's commands?

_____ Yes _____ No

Do the people honor the Word of God, or do they worship other gods? Circle the one that fits your country:

Honor God's Word   Worship other gods

Name a sin that is obvious in your country.

____

A Second Chance   85

WHAT should you do for your country?

____

Now say your memory verse. WHAT are the men to do? WHAT are they to call on or pray to God and ask? Do that for your country so that it may turn from its wicked ways and God won't have to judge your country.

Tomorrow we will finish our investigation so we can scoop the competition with our story. Way to go!

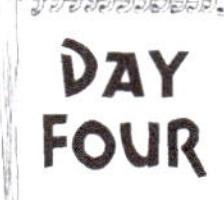

DAY FOUR

COVERING THE STORY

92 You did a great job yesterday finding out how the people in Nineveh reacted to Jonah's message. Were you surprised when they fasted and put on sackcloth to show their sorrow over their sin? How will God respond to their actions?

Let's find out by heading back to Nineveh to see what God does so we can write a story for the next edition. Don't forget to talk to God.

Turn to page 125. Read Jonah 3 and mark the following key words on your Observation Worksheets. Add any new key words to your key-word bookmark.

deeds (draw and color green feet)

calamity (draw a blue wavy line under the word and red lines like this over the word and color the word red)

Great! Let's make a list on what we've learned about God.

(page 85)

(page 125)

Chapter 3

1 Now the word of the LORD came to Jonah the second time, saying,

2 "Arise, go to Nineveh the great city and proclaim to it the proclamation which I am going to tell you."

3 So Jonah arose and went to Nineveh according to the word of the LORD. Now Nineveh was an exceedingly great city, a three days' walk.

4 Then Jonah began to go through the city one day's walk; and he cried out and said, "Yet forty days and Nineveh will be overthrown."

5 Then the people of Nineveh believed in God; and they called a fast and put on sackcloth from the greatest to the least of them.

6 When the word reached the king of Nineveh, he arose from his throne, laid aside his robe from him, covered himself with sackcloth and sat on the ashes.

(page 126)

7 He issued a proclamation and it said, "In Nineveh by the decree of the king and his nobles: Do not let man, beast, herd, or flock taste a thing. Do not let them eat or drink water.

8 "But both man and beast must be covered with sackcloth; and let men call on God earnestly that each may turn from his wicked way and from the violence which is in his hands.

9 "Who knows, God may turn and relent and withdraw His burning anger so that we will not perish."

10 When God saw their deeds, that they turned from their wicked way, then God relented concerning the calamity which He had declared He would bring upon them. And He did not do it.

Guided Instruction

DAY FOUR

Ask God to give you clear understanding of this lesson.

92 Turn to page 85 and read "Covering the Story."

Add new key words to your bookmark. Reread Jonah 3 aloud as students follow along and call out the key words as you mark them together as we noted on page 16.

Deeds (draw and color green feet)

Calamity (draw a clue wavy line under the word and red lines over the word and color the word red)

Guided Instruction

93 List what you learned about God on page 86.

What I Learned About God

Jonah 3:1 The Lord gives His w <u>o</u> <u>r</u> <u>d</u> to Jonah a <u>second</u> time.

Jonah 3:2–4 The Lord gives Jonah the <u>proclamation</u> that in <u>forty</u> days God will <u>overthrow</u> Nineveh.

Jonah 3:9 God may <u>turn</u> and <u>relent</u> and withdraw His burning <u>anger</u>.

Jonah 3:10 God saw the people of Nineveh's <u>deeds</u>. God r <u>e</u> <u>l</u> <u>e</u> <u>n</u> <u>t</u> <u>e</u> <u>d</u> concerning the <u>calamity</u> which He had declared He would bring upon them. And He did not do it.

94 Read and discuss the text on pages 86-87.

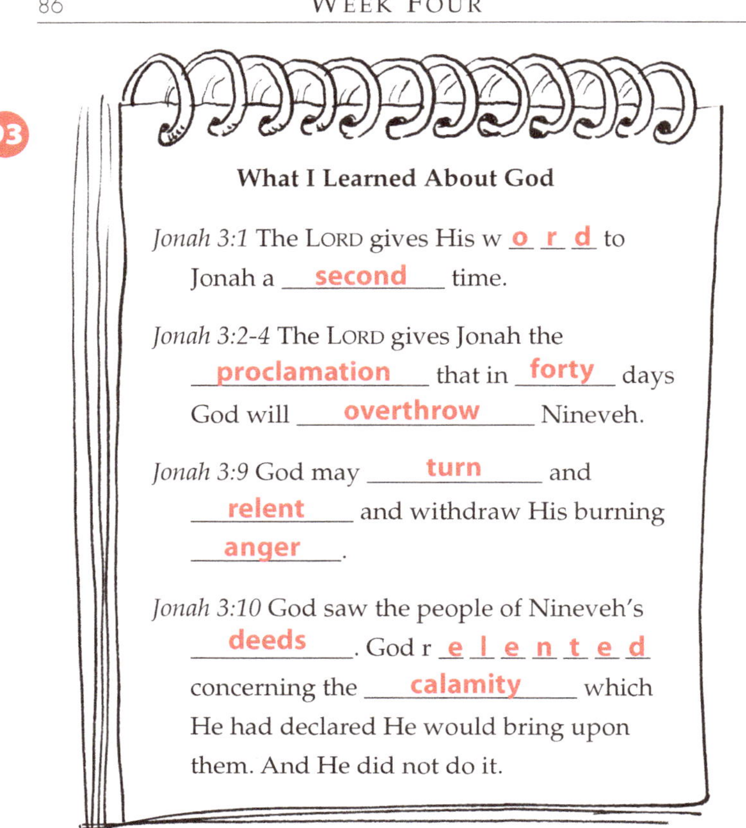

Wow! Look at what we learned about God. God gives His word to Jonah a second time. This shows us that God is a God of second chances. He doesn't give up on us when we make a mistake or fail. He is going to help us accomplish His will.

God is all-powerful! He can destroy a city. God appoints time—He decides when something will happen.

And God may change His mind. God changed His mind about destroying Nineveh. In Exodus 32:9-14, God was going to destroy the children of Israel because of their sin. Moses pleaded with

God and asked Him not to destroy them. Moses reminded God of His promises to His people, and God changed His mind. God listens when we pray! He sees our hearts, and He may change His mind.

God gets angry over sin. His anger is a *righteous* (right and just) anger.

God saw the deeds of the people in Nineveh. In Hebrew, one of God's names is *El Roi*, which means "God sees." God sees when we do what is right and when we do what is wrong. God sees our hearts. He sees everything!

God relented about the calamity He was going to bring on Nineveh. *Relent* means "to be sorry" or "change your mind" or "to repent." God changed His mind about destroying the city. God is merciful.

 Look at Jonah 3:10. WHY would God change His mind about destroying Nineveh and its people?

They turned from their wicked way.

That is so awesome! God saw the people of Nineveh's deeds. God saw how sorry they were for their sins. He saw their actions (what they did to show they were sorry). God saw they believed Him because they repented; they changed their behavior and turned to Him. So God changed His mind about destroying them. God did not give the people of Nineveh what they deserved.

Look up and read Romans 3:23 in your Bible.

WHAT have we all done? We have all ______**sinned**______ and fall ______**short**______ of the glory of God.

Look up and read Romans 6:23.

WHAT is the wages of sin? **Death**

WHAT is the free gift from God?
Eternal life

Jonah 3:10 WHY would God change His mind about destroying Nineveh and its people? They turned from their wicked way.

Read the selected scriptures to answer the questions.

Romans 3:23 WHAT have we all done? We have all sinned and fall short of the glory of God.

Roman 6:23 WHAT is the wages of sin? Death

WHAT is the free gift from God? Eternal life

Guided Instruction

Romans 5:6–11 HOW did God demonstrate His love toward us?

Christt died for us.

 Read and discuss the rest of the text for lesson four.

Practice saying the memory verse with a friend.

---

and ask, *Am I obeying God the first time? Am I obeying the people God has put in authority over me—my parents and teachers? Am I pleasing God with my deeds or actions?* (God only expects you to obey those in authority over you as long as they are not hurting you or asking you to do something that is wrong.)

If you see anything that you need to change, go to God and tell Him how sorry you are. Ask Him to help you. As a follower of Jesus, you are to lay aside your old self and put on the new self, which is in the likeness of God (Ephesians 4:22-24). You are to be like Jesus and obey God the first time!

All right! Tomorrow we will proof our story. Don't forget to practice your memory verse.

Guided Instruction

Ask God to bring the details to your mind so that you can write the story.

97 Turn to page 89 and read "Type and Proof."

(page 89)

97

TYPE AND PROOF

"Look, Molly! Look at Sam. He has an envelope tied around his neck. Let's see if there's a letter inside."

"Okay!" Molly cut the string and opened the envelope. "Yes! It's a note from Mr. Chase. He wants us to proof our story right away so we can finish in time for the next edition to go to print."

"I'm ready. I have my copy. Do you have yours?" Max said.

"I'll print it out." Molly hit the print button and walked over to get her news story about Nineveh.

"I'll pray," Max said, "and then we can get started."

Okay, rookie reporter, grab your red pen so you can proof your copy.

Turn to page 125 and read Jonah 3.

WHAT is your story about? Write an eye-catching headline at the top of the newspaper.

WHAT is the weather like in Nineveh? Jonah 3 doesn't tell us, but we know that the weather in this country is usually sunny and sizzling hot. Be the weather forecaster for the *Nineveh News* and predict what the weather might be like. Draw a picture of your weather forecast in the weather corner on the newspaper.

(page 125)

Chapter 3

1 Now the word of the L ORD came to Jonah the second time, saying,

2 "Arise, go to Nineveh the great city and proclaim to it the proclamation which I am going to tell you."

3 So Jonah arose and went to Nineveh according to the word of the L ORD. Now Nineveh was an exceedingly great city, a three days' walk.

4 Then Jonah began to go through the city one day's walk; and he cried out and said, "Yet forty days and Nineveh will be overthrown."

5 Then the people of Nineveh believed in God; and they called a fast and put on sackcloth from the greatest to the least of them.

6 When the word reached the king of Nineveh, he arose from his throne, laid aside his robe from him, covered himself with sackcloth and sat on the ashes.

(page 126)

7 He issued a proclamation and it said, "In Nineveh by the decree of the king and his nobles: Do not let man, beast, herd, or flock taste a thing. Do not let them eat or drink water.

8 "But both man and beast must be covered with sackcloth; and let men call on God earnestly that each may turn from his wicked way and from the violence which is in his hands.

9 "Who knows, God may turn and relent and withdraw His burning anger so that we will not perish."

10 When God saw their deeds, that they turned from their wicked way, then God relented concerning the calamity which He had declared He would bring upon them. And He did not do it.

Now proof your news story by filling in each of the blanks on your newspaper.

WHAT scene in Jonah 3 do you think will get your readers' attention? Draw a picture to capture the action.

98

NINEVEH NEWS

ISSUE 4

BREAKING NEWS!

Sunny

Weather   **Jonah goes to Nineveh**
(Put your headline here)

After the great fish vomits Jonah onto dry land, the **Lord** WHO (Jonah 3:1) tells Jonah a **second** WHAT (Jonah 3:1) time to go to **Nineveh** WHERE (verse 2) to tell the people that in 40 days the great city will be **overthrown** WHAT (verse 4). The people listen to Jonah's message and call on God. They call for a **fast** WHAT (Jonah 3:5) and put on **sackcloth** WHAT (Jonah 3:5). When word reaches the **king** WHO (Jonah 3:6), he gets up from his throne and lays aside his robe to cover himself with sackcloth and sit on the ashes. Immediately the king tells all the people and the animals not to **eat** WHAT (Jonah 3:7) or **drink** WHAT (Jonah 3:7) water. They must

DRAW A PICTURE

cover themselves with sackcloth and call on God. The king also says that each one must turn from his wicked ways so that God may turn and withdraw His burning anger so they will not perish. God sees their d **e e d** s, changes His mind, and does not bring the **calamity** WHAT (Jonah 3:10) upon them. God saves Nineveh!

Guided Instruction

98 Transfer the format of "Nineveh News, Issue 4" to large chart paper. As students reread Jonah 3 fill in the chart and have them complete page 90.

NINEVEH NEWS

ISSUE 4

BREAKING NEWS!

(headline) **Jonah goes to Nineveh**

WEATHER:

Sunny

After the great fish vomits Jonah onto dry land, the **Lord** tells Jonah a **second** time to go to **Nineveh** to tell the people that in 40 days the great city will be **overthrown**. The people listen to Jonah's message and call on God. They call for a **fast** and put on **sackcloth**. When word reaches the **king**, he gets up from his throne and lays aside his robe to cover himself with sackcloth and sit on the ashes. Immediately the king tells all the people and the animals not to **eat** or **drink** water. They must cover themselves with sackcloth and call on God. The king also says that each one must turn from his wicked ways so that God may turn and withdraw His burning anger so they will not perish. God sees their d **e e d** s, changes His mind, and does not bring the **calamity** upon them. God saves Nineveh!

Guided Instruction

 Read "Roll the Presses!" "Extra! Extra!" and "Sackcloth" on page 91.

Continue acting out the scenes in Jonah 3.

Say the memory verse to an adult.

Use the quiz on Week Four on page 141 to check memory and understanding

You may also want to play a game for the kids to review what they have learned.

ROLL THE PRESSES!

Great copy, rookie reporter! We are ready to print! Wasn't it an incredible week as you watched the wicked people in Nineveh turn away from their sins? Have you ever been around kids or grown-ups that you didn't think could or would ever listen or change? What if you told them about Jesus and they did change—would that make you happy? How do you think Jonah feels now that Nineveh has been saved? We'll find out as we track down the answers next week!

Don't forget to say your memory verse to a grown-up.

"EXTRA! EXTRA!"

It's time to pick up where we left off in acting out Jonah's story. There are a lot of new characters to add to your cast this week. Get some friends or family members to play the people in Nineveh and the king. Borrow a robe from your mom or dad for the king. You can make a crown out of construction paper and tape. Get some bread and water but don't eat or drink it. And don't forget to have someone make animal noises for all the hungry animals in this awesome scene.

Sackcloth

If you really want to experience what it would feel like to wear sackcloth, maybe a grown-up could get you a feed sack from a feed-and-seed store.

Then cut a round hole at the bottom of the feed sack for your head to go through and a hole on each side of the sack for your arms. Slide the sack over your head and wear it like a tunic. This really itchy and scratchy sack is a good sackcloth substitute. Now, get back inside your great fish and start by acting out being vomited onto the beach.

You Are Invited!

Another cool thing you can do is be a missionary like Jonah in

---

your neighborhood or school. Invite a kid or kids to an event at your church. Or you could invite them over to your house and do one of these inductive Bible studies with them. Give them their own books and colored pencils, have a snack, and just hang out with them when you are finished.

JONAH 4

Can you believe this is our last week at *Nineveh News?* We have learned so much! Last week we arrived in Nineveh and watched the wrong-way prophet finally go the right way by proclaiming God's message to the people of Nineveh.

We also saw the people of Nineveh hear God's message and repent of what they were doing wrong. An awesome God decides to save the people and the city. HOW do you think Jonah feels about God saving Nineveh? HOW would you feel if God saved one of your enemies?

Let's head back to Nineveh and track down Jonah to find out what happens next.

TRACKING THE STORY

 **100** "Molly, come look at this. Sam is trying to answer the phone. He wants to be the first to hear the latest news."

"I'll answer it," Molly offered. "No telling what Sam will do if he gets ahold of that phone. He would probably chew it to pieces."

93

WEEK 5

God is teaching Jonah that His commands are very serious. Ask God to strengthen you to obey Him.

100 Turn to page 93 and read "Jonah 4" and "Tracking the Story."

Guided Instruction

101 Turn to page 126 and read Jonah 4 aloud as students follow along and call out the key words as you mark them together as we noted on page 16.

God (Lord) (draw a purple triangle and color it yellow)

Jonah (color it orange)

Prayed (draw a purple bowl and color it pink)

Angry (anger) (draw a black squiggly line through the word)

Calamity (draw a blue wavy line under the word, red lines over it, and color it red)

WHERE (underline in green words that denote place)

WHEN (draw a green clock over words that denote time)

---

94   WEEK FIVE

"Yeah, you're right," Max agreed. "He has gotten into a lot of stuff. I think Sam loves being a reporter."

"He sure does—maybe a little too much." Molly rescued the phone from Sam and listened carefully. Then she hung up. "That was Mr. Chase, Max. He wants us to track down Jonah now that Nineveh has been saved. We need to get more facts to wrap up our story."

"I'll pray," Max said, as he patted Sam. "Then we can get right on it."

Okay, rookie reporter, now that you have talked to God, are you ready to head back to Nineveh and track down Jonah? Great! Grab those colored pencils and turn to page 126.

Read Jonah 4 and mark the following key words on your Observation Worksheets.

God (Lord) (draw a purple triangle and color it yellow)

Jonah (color it orange)

prayed (draw a purple [bowl] and color it pink)

angry (anger) (draw a black squiggly line like this: ⋀⋀⋀)

calamity (draw a blue wavy line under the word and red lines like this ⋀⋀⋀ over the word and color the word red)

(page 126)

would bring upon them. And He did not do it.

Chapter 4

1 But it greatly displeased Jonah and he became angry.

2 He prayed to the LORD and said, "Please LORD, was not this what I said while I was still in my own country? Therefore in order to forestall this I fled to Tarshish, for I knew that You are a gracious and compassionate God, slow to anger and abundant in lovingkindness, and one who relents concerning calamity.

3 "Therefore now, O LORD, please take my life from me, for death is better to me than life."

4 The LORD said, "Do you have good reason to be angry?"

5 Then Jonah went out from the city and sat east of it. There he made a shelter for himself and sat under it in the shade until he could see what would happen in the city.

6 So the LORD God appointed a plant and it grew up over Jonah to be a shade over his head to deliver him from his discomfort. And Jonah was extremely happy about the plant.

7 But God appointed a worm when dawn came the next day and it attacked the plant and it withered.

8 When the sun came up God appointed a scorching east wind, and the sun beat down on Jonah's head so that he became faint and begged with all his soul to die, saying, "Death is better to me than life."

9 Then God said to Jonah, "Do you have good reason to be angry about the plant?" And he said, "I have good reason to be angry, even to death."

10 Then the LORD said, "You had compassion on the plant for which you did not work and which you did not cause to grow, which came up overnight and perished overnight.

11 "Should I not have compassion on Nineveh, the great city in which there are more than 120,000 persons who do not know the difference between their right and left hand, as well as many animals?"

Guided Instruction

102 Reread the selected verses to answer the questions.

Jonah 4:1 HOW does Jonah feel, and WHAT does he become? He is displeased and becomes angry.

WHAT is Jonah angry about? Look back at Jonah 3:10. WHAT didn't God do that He said He was going to do? God didn't punish Nineveh.

Jonah 4:2 WHY did Jonah flee to Tarshish? WHY didn't Jonah want to go to Nineveh? He knew God would relent of His anger if the people turned from their wicked ways.

103 Discuss the meaning of "forestall."

Jonah 4:2 WHAT did Jonah know about God that made him think God would relent and save Nineveh? "You are a gracious and compassionate God, slow to anger and abundant in lovingkindness, and one who relents concerning calamity."

An Angry Prophet   95

Don't forget to mark the pronouns! And mark anything that tells you WHERE by double-underlining the WHERE in green. Mark anything that tells you WHEN by drawing a green clock or green circle: .

Now get the details. Be a good reporter and ask those 5 W's and an H.

102

Jonah 4:1 HOW does Jonah feel, and WHAT does he become?

He is displeased and becomes angry.

WHAT is Jonah angry about? Look back at Jonah 3:10. WHAT didn't God do that He said He was going to do?

God didn't punish Nineveh.

Jonah 4:2 WHY did Jonah flee to Tarshish? WHY didn't Jonah want to go to Nineveh?

He knew God would relent of His anger if the people turned from their wicked ways.

103 Do you know what that word *forestall* means? To forestall means to put something off, to keep it from happening. Jonah was trying to put off going to Nineveh because he didn't want God to save the people or the city.

Jonah 4:2 WHAT did Jonah know about God that made him think God might relent and save Nineveh?

"You are a _gracious_ and _compassionate_ God, _slow_ to _anger_ and abundant in _lovingkindness_, and one who _relents_ concerning _calamity_."

WEEK FIVE

96

Jonah knew God's character. Jonah knew that God was kind and compassionate, and that God might relent concerning destroying Nineveh—and all the people and animals in it.

Let's contrast Jonah's reaction to the situation with God's response. A *contrast* shows how two things are different or opposite, such as light and dark or truth and lie.

Look at the two verses below and list the words that describe Jonah in Jonah 4:1 and God in Jonah 4:2. HOW are their reactions different?

Jonah	**God**
Jonah 4:1	Jonah 4:2
Displeased	Gracious
Angry	Compassionate
	Slow to anger,
	Abundant in lovingkindness

WHAT a difference! WHO are you most like, Jonah or God?

____

All right! What else does Jonah say to God in his prayer? How will God answer? You'll find out as you get back on the story tomorrow. Before you leave, let's discover this week's memory verse.

Look at the plant. Start at the bottom and follow the words up as the plant grows tall. As you come to each word inside a leaf, unscramble it and write it in the next blank in the verse under the plant.

Guided Instruction

104 Discuss God's character. Then contrast Jonah's reaction with God's response.

JONAH	GOD
Jonah 4:1	Jonah 4:2
Displeased	Gracious
Angry	Compassionate
	Slow to anger,
	Abundant in lovingkindness

Discuss the next question and have students answer it independently.

Guided Instruction

105 Look at the plant on page 97 and discover the memory verse.

"You are a <u>gracious</u> and <u>compassionate</u> God, <u>slow</u> to <u>anger</u> and <u>abundant</u> in <u>lovingkindness</u>, and one who <u>relents</u> concerning <u>calamity</u>."

Jonah 4:<u>2</u>

Copy the memory verse to an index card and practice saying it three times, three times a day.

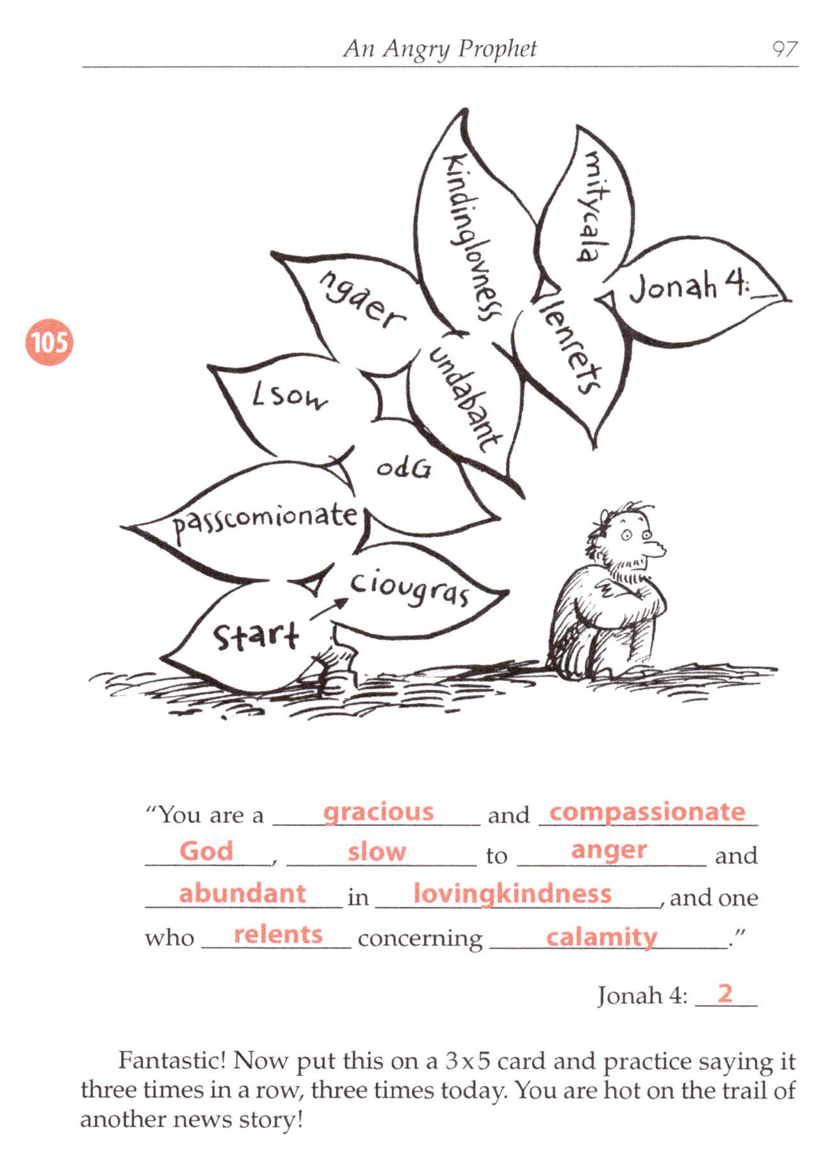

"You are a ______gracious______ and ______compassionate______ ______God______, ______slow______ to ______anger______ and ______abundant______ in ______lovingkindness______, and one who ______relents______ concerning ______calamity______."

Jonah 4: ___2___

Fantastic! Now put this on a 3 x 5 card and practice saying it three times in a row, three times today. You are hot on the trail of another news story!

106 ## GATHER THE FACTS

Can you believe that Jonah got angry because God saved Nineveh? Were you surprised when God's prophet prayed and told God why he didn't want to go to Nineveh? What will happen next? How will God respond to Jonah's prayer? Let's find out. Don't forget to pray.

107 Now turn to page 126. Read Jonah 4 and gather the facts.

Guided Instruction

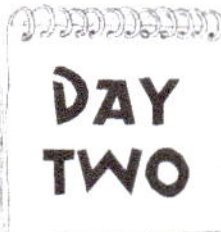

Ask God to place in your heart any changes you need to make in your life.

106 Turn to page 98 and read "Gather the Facts."

107 Turn to page 126 and reread the selected verses to answer the questions on pages 98–101.

Guided Instruction

(page 126)

would bring upon them. And He did not do it.

Chapter 4

1 But it greatly displeased Jonah and he became angry.

2 He prayed to the LORD and said, "Please LORD, was not this what I said while I was still in my own country? Therefore in order to forestall this I fled to Tarshish, for I knew that You are a gracious and compassionate God, slow to anger and abundant in lovingkindness, and one who relents concerning calamity.

3 "Therefore now, O LORD, please take my life from me, for death is better to me than life."

4 The LORD said, "Do you have good reason to be angry?"

5 Then Jonah went out from the city and sat east of it. There he made a shelter for himself and sat under it in the shade until he could see what would happen in the city.

6 So the LORD God appointed a plant and it grew up over Jonah to be a shade over his head to deliver him from his discomfort. And Jonah was extremely happy about the plant.

7 But God appointed a worm when dawn came the next day and it attacked the plant and it withered.

8 When the sun came up God appointed a scorching east wind, and the sun beat down on Jonah's head so that he became faint and begged with all his soul to die, saying, "Death is better to me than life."

9 Then God said to Jonah, "Do you have good reason to be angry about the plant?" And he said, "I have good reason to be angry, even to death."

10 Then the LORD said, "You had compassion on the plant for which you did not work and which you did not cause to grow, which came up overnight and perished overnight.

11 "Should I not have compassion on Nineveh, the great city in which there are more than 120,000 persons who do not know the difference between their right and left hand, as well as many animals?"

(page 98)

Jonah 4:3 WHAT else does Jonah say to God in his prayer?

"Take my life from me, for death is better to me than life."

An Angry Prophet   99

Jonah 4:4 WHAT does God ask Jonah?

Do you have a good reason to be angry?

Jonah 4:5 HOW does Jonah answer God? Does he say anything to God?

_____ Yes   __X__ No

WHERE does Jonah go?

Out from the city

WHAT does Jonah do?

Sits in the shade of a shelter

HOW long does Jonah sit there? WHAT is he waiting to see?

He's waiting to see what God will do to Nineveh.

108 That's pretty unbelievable, isn't it? Does Jonah have a good attitude or a bad attitude? Circle the answer.

Good attitude   (Bad attitude)

In verse 3, Jonah is soooo angry that he tells God to take his life. He would rather be dead. Isn't that sad? Jonah would rather be dead than to see the Ninevites saved. HOW does God respond?

In verse 4, WHAT did God ask Jonah?

"Do you have ______**good**______ ______**reason**______ to be ______**angry**______?"

Now think about when you get angry. Ask, "Do I get angry when things don't go my way or someone doesn't do what I want them to do? Or do I get angry because I have a good reason?" Write

Guided Instruction

Jonah 4:3 WHAT else does Jonah say to God in his prayer? "Take my life from me, for death is better to me than life."

Jonah 4:4 WHAT does God ask Jonah? Do you have a good reason to be angry?

Jonah 4:5 HOW does Jonah answer God? Does he say anything to God? No

WHERE does Jonah go? Out from the city

WHAT does Jonah do? Sits in the shade of a shelter

HOW long does Jonah sit there? WHAT is he waiting to see? He's waiting to see what God will do to Nineveh.

108 Discuss "attitude" and circle the answer to the next question.

Jonah is so angry he doesn't want God to save the Ninevites. **WHAT did God ask Jonah?** Jonah 4:4 "Do you have good reason to be angry?"

Guided Instruction

(109) Lead a discussion about anger and have students answer independently on page 100.

Read the selected verses to answer the questions.

Jonah 3:8–9 WHAT makes God angry?
Wickedness and violence

Jonah 4:8–9 WHAT makes Jonah angry? The plant withered and he was scorched by the wind and the sun.

Jonah 4:9 WHAT question does God ask Jonah this time? "Do you have good reason to be angry?"

HOW did Jonah respond to God? "I have good reason, even to death."

---

100   WEEK FIVE

(109) out WHAT happened the last time you got angry. Tell what your reason was—and whether it was a good reason to be angry.

____

____

____

____

Have you ever been so mad that you just stomped off? Did you sit down and fold your arms and pout? The next time you get angry, instead of stomping off, stop and talk to God about it. Tell Him why you are angry. Ask Him what He wants you to do.

Since anger is a very important key word in Jonah 4 and a powerful emotion, let's find out what else makes Jonah angry and compare it to what makes God angry.

Turn to page 126. Read Jonah 3:8-9.

Jonah 3:8-9 WHAT makes God angry?

_______ Wickedness _______ and _______ violence _______

Turn to page 126. Read Jonah 4:7-9.

Jonah 4:8 WHAT makes Jonah angry?

The plant withered and he was scorched by the wind and the sun.

Jonah 4:9 WHAT question does God ask Jonah this time?

"Do you have good reason to be angry?"

HOW did Jonah respond to God?

"I have good reason, even to death."

Can you believe that Jonah gets this angry over a plant that dies? Does Jonah have a good reason to be angry over a plant (a thing)?

Let's look at a few cross-references to see what God has to say about anger. Look up and read Ephesians 4:26-27.

Ephesians 4:26 WHAT does this verse say about anger?

"Be angry, and *yet* do not sin."

That means it is okay to be angry as long as you aren't sinning in your anger. Are you to stay angry? WHAT does it say?

"Do not let the **sun** go down on your **anger** ."

That means we are *not* to stomp off, slam the door, pout, and stay mad. We are to get over our anger before the day ends. Did Jonah run off when he got angry? ____ Yes ____ No

Did Jonah sin in his anger? ____ Yes ____ No

Ephesians 4:27 WHAT happens when you don't deal with your anger God's way?

You give the devil opportunity.

Read Ephesians 4:31-32.

Ephesians 4:31 WHAT six things are you to put away?

Bitterness, wrath, anger, clamor, slander, and malice

Ephesians 4:32 WHAT are you to do?

"Be **kind** to one another, **tender**-**hearted** , **forgiving** each other, just as God in **Christ** also has **forgiven** **you** ."

Read the selected cross-references to answer the questions about anger.

Ephesians 4:26 WHAT does this verse say about anger? "Be angry, and *yet* do not sin."

WHAT else does it say? "Do not let the sun go down on your anger."

Lead a discussion about the next two questions.

Ephesians 4:27 WHAT happens when you don't deal with your anger God's way? You give the devil opportunity.

Ephesians 4:31–32 WHAT six things are you to put away? Bitterness, wrath, anger, clamor, slander, and malice

Ephesians 4:32 WHAT are you to do? "Be kind to one another, tender-hearted, forgiving each other, just as God in Christ also has forgiven you."

Lead a discussion about the rest of the text.

Practice saying the memory verse with a friend.

Guided Instruction

Way to go! You have seen that Jonah was angry because a plant died that was giving him some comfort. But God's anger was because the people of Nineveh were sinning, hurting each other, and worshipping idols. And even though God had every reason to wipe Nineveh out, He was kind and compassionate. But when Jonah got mad, he stomped off. Jonah did not have a good reason to be angry, but God sure did!

The next time you get angry, remember what you learned in Ephesians. Ask, "Am I acting like Jonah? Am I angry over not having my way or about things like the plant? Or am I angry because of someone's sin? Am I acting the way God wants me to act?"

Your memory verse this week has something to say about getting angry. Why don't you practice saying it out loud three times in a row today to remind you to be slow to get angry?

Great work!

(page 102)

DAY THREE

110

TRACKING DOWN GOD

Yesterday as you gathered the facts, you learned what made Jonah and God angry. Today you need to stay on the story by getting a closer look at God. You have seen how loving and compassionate God is. Get the complete story in Jonah 4. Find out WHAT God does. Don't forget to ask for your "Master Editor's" help.

Turn to page 126. Read Jonah 4 and mark the following key word on your Observation Worksheets.

appointed (color it green)

Get all the facts about what God does by making a list in your notebook. First read Jonah 1:17 and list what God does. Now turn to Jonah 4 on page 126 and finish your list.

(page 126)

would bring upon them. And He did not do it.

Chapter 4

1 But it greatly displeased Jonah and he became angry.

2 He prayed to the LORD and said, "Please LORD, was not this what I said while I was still in my own country? Therefore in order to forestall this I fled to Tarshish, for I knew that You are a gracious and compassionate God, slow to anger and abundant in lovingkindness, and one who relents concerning calamity.

3 "Therefore now, O LORD, please take my life from me, for death is better to me than life."

4 The LORD said, "Do you have good reason to be angry?"

5 Then Jonah went out from the city and sat east of it. There he made a shelter for himself and sat under it in the shade until he could see what would happen in the city.

6 So the LORD God appointed a plant and it grew up over Jonah to be a shade over his head to deliver him from his discomfort. And Jonah was extremely happy about the plant.

7 But God appointed a worm when dawn came the next day and it attacked the plant and it withered.

DAY THREE

Ask God to give you a special message today.

110 Turn to page 102 and read "Tracking Down God."

Reread Jonah 4 and mark another key word.

Appointed (color it green)

Guided Instruction

111 List facts about God on page 103.

WHAT God Does

Jonah 1:17 The Lord <u>appointed</u> a great <u>fish</u> to <u>swallow</u> Jonah.

Jonah 4:6 The Lord God <u>appointed</u> a <u>plant</u>.

Jonah 4:7 God <u>appointed</u> a <u>worm</u>.

Jonah 4:8 God <u>appointed</u> a <u>scorching</u> <u>east</u> <u>wind</u>.

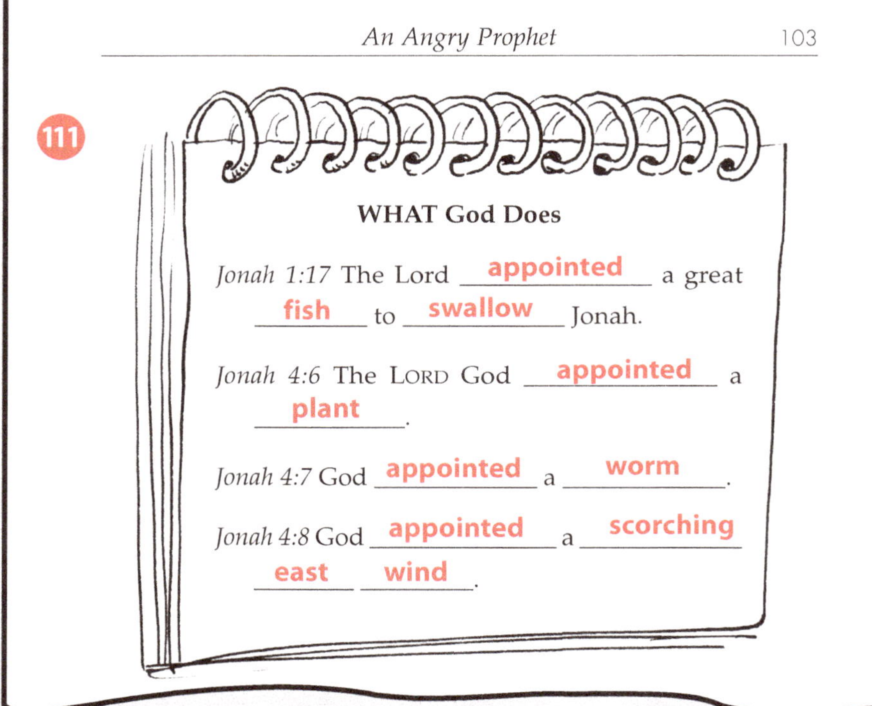

(page 103)

Draw a picture in the box of the four things God appointed.

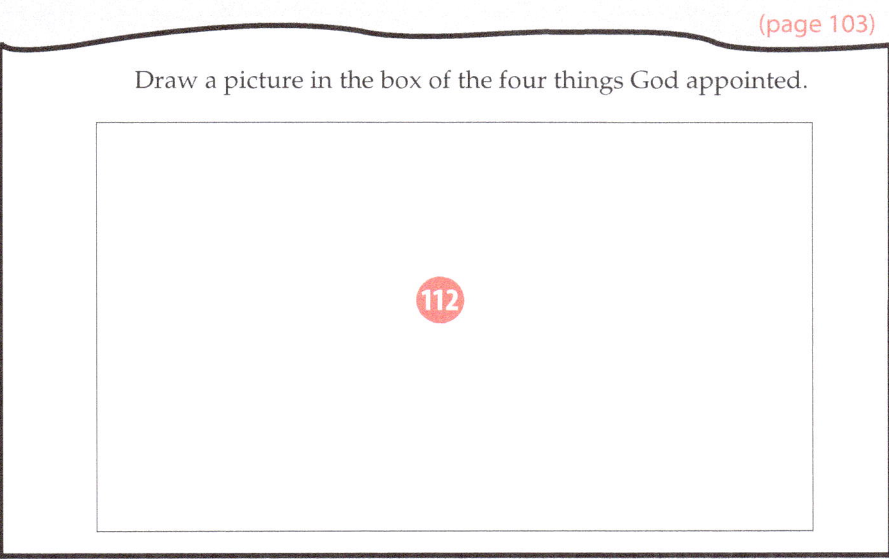

Guided Instruction

 **112** Draw a picture of these four things God appointed.

Jonah 4:6 WHY did God appoint the plant? To give Jonah shade

113 Draw a happy, sad, or angry face to show how Jonah feels about the plant.

Jonah 4:7 WHY did God appoint the worm? To attack the plant

Jonah 4:8 WHY did God appoint the scorching wind? WHAT did the sun do? It beat down on Jonah's head.

Practice saying the memory verse to a friend.

---

104   WEEK FIVE

Isn't that exciting? Now let's find out WHY God appointed these things. We already know God appointed the great fish to save Jonah's life.

Jonah 4:6 WHY did God appoint the plant?

To give Jonah shade

HOW did Jonah feel about the plant? Draw a happy, sad, or angry face to show this.

113

Jonah 4:7 WHY did God appoint the worm?

To attack the plant

Jonah 4:8 WHY did God appoint the scorching wind? WHAT did the sun do?

It beat down on Jonah's head.

Wow! You have just seen some awesome things about God and creation. God not only made these things, He is over them. He is in charge. God is in control of nature. He appoints. God has a specific task for each one of these creations to bring about His plan in Jonah's life.

Isn't that astounding? God is the ruler over everything! God is sovereign.

Don't forget to practice your memory verse!

Guided Instruction

Jonah was more concerned for himself than for others. Ask God to give you a heart of compassion for others.

114 Turn to page 105 and read "A Nose for News."

115 Reread Jonah 4 and mark the following key word.

Compassion (compassionate) (color it pink)

A NOSE FOR NEWS

114 "Hey, Max, wasn't it cool learning that God appointed the great fish, the plant, the worm, and the scorching wind—that God is sovereign and has a plan for all those things?" Molly asked.

"It sure was." Max nodded. "We know what happened when God appointed all those things, but I wonder what God wanted to teach Jonah?"

Molly jumped up, excited. "That's what we need to find out to finish our news story. WHAT did God want the plant, the worm, and the wind to accomplish? WHAT did God want to teach Jonah? We better grab our notebooks. We don't have much time left before we have to write this story."

Okay, rookie reporter, let's wrap up this last news story. Don't forget to talk to God.

Turn to page 126. Read Jonah 4 and mark the following key word on your Observation Worksheets.

compassion (compassionate) (color it pink)

Now, let's uncover the rest of the facts. Let's compare Jonah's compassion to God's compassion.

would bring upon them. And He did not do it.

(page 126)

115 Chapter 4

1 But it greatly displeased Jonah and he became angry.

2 He prayed to the LORD and said, "Please LORD, was not this what I said while I was still in my own country? Therefore in order to forestall this I fled to Tarshish, for I knew that You are a gracious and compassionate God, slow to anger and abundant in lovingkindness, and one who relents concerning calamity.

3 "Therefore now, O LORD, please take my life from me, for death is better to me than life."

4 The LORD said, "Do you have good reason to be angry?"

5 Then Jonah went out from the city and sat east of it. There he made a shelter for himself and sat under it in the shade until he could see what would happen in the city.

6 So the LORD God appointed a plant and it grew up over Jonah to be a shade over his head to deliver him from his discomfort. And Jonah was extremely happy about the plant.

7 But God appointed a worm when dawn came the next day and it attacked the plant and it withered.

Observation Worksheets—Jonah   127

8 When the sun came up God appointed a scorching east wind, and the sun beat down on Jonah's head so that he became faint and begged with all his soul to die, saying, "Death is better to me than life."

9 Then God said to Jonah, "Do you have good reason to be angry about the plant?" And he said, "I have good reason to be angry, even to death."

10 Then the LORD said, "You had compassion on the plant for which you did not work and which you did not cause to grow, which came up over-night and perished overnight.

11 "Should I not have compassion on Nineveh, the great city in which there are more than 120,000 persons who do not know the difference between their right and left hand, as well as many animals?"

(page 105)

compassion to God's compassion.

116

Jonah 4:10 WHAT did Jonah have compassion on?

The plant

Jonah 4:6. WHY was Jonah compassionate about the plant? WHAT did the plant do?

It provided shade for Jonah.

106   WEEK FIVE

WHERE is Jonah's focus: on himself or others?

Himself

Jonah 4:11 WHAT did God have compassion on?

116 Read the selected verses to answer the questions.

Jonah 4:10 WHAT did Jonah have compassion on? **The plant**

Jonah 4:6 WHY was Jonah compassionate about the plant? WHAT did the plant do? **It provided shade for Jonah.**

WHERE was Jonah's focus: on himself or on others? **Himself**

Guided Instruction

Jonah 4:11 WHAT did God have compassion on? Nineveh

Lead a discussion about the next two questions and have students answer them independently.

Jonah 4:11 WHY is God compassionate to Nineveh? WHAT do you learn about the people? They did not know the difference between their right and left hands.

Lead a discussion about Jonah and answer the questions.

Read the selected verses in cross-references and answer the questions.

John 3:16 WHAT did God do for the world? He gave His only begotten son.

WHY? To save us so we would not perish

2 Peter 3:9 WHY is God patient? He does not want anyone to perish.

WHAT does God want for all people? To come to repentance

Lead a discussion about the next questions.

Read the selected verses Matthew 5:44–48, Romans 12:14–21, and 1 John 3:10 to answer the questions.

(page 106)

Jonah 4:11 WHAT did God have compassion on?

Nineveh

Which is more important? Should we have compassion for things or compassion for people?

Jonah's attitude is pretty shocking, isn't it? Jonah is compassionate about something that makes *him* comfortable, but God cares about *people* and whether they live or die.

HOW about you? WHAT are you compassionate about?

Jonah 4:11. WHY is God compassionate to Nineveh? WHAT do you learn about the people?

They did not know the difference between their right and left hands.

An Angry Prophet   107

Did Jonah care about the people in Nineveh?

____ Yes   __X__ No

Should he have cared?

__X__ Yes   ____ No

WHAT is God's heart toward those who are sinners? Pull out your Bible and look up and read John 3:16.

John 3:16 WHAT did God do for the world?

He gave His only begotten son.

WHY? To save us so we would not perish

God loves people so much that He gave His Son to die for our sins!

Look up and read 2 Peter 3:9.

2 Peter 3:9 WHY is God patient?

He does not want anyone to perish.

WHAT does God want for all people?

To come to repentance

(page 107)

God was patient toward the Ninevites because He doesn't want anyone to perish! Jonah didn't want God to save the Ninevites. Jonah wanted God to punish them! Are you surprised? Have you ever wanted God to punish someone you didn't like?

____ Yes   ____ No

WHAT should your attitude be toward other people? Let's find out.

---

108   WEEK FIVE

Look up and read Matthew 5:44-48.

Matthew 5:44 HOW are you to treat your enemies?

Love enemies; pray for those who persecute me.

Look up and read Romans 12:14-21.

Romans 12:14 WHAT are we to do to those who persecute us?
Bless them

Romans 12:20 HOW are we to treat our enemies?

Feed them if they're hungry and give them a drink if they are thirsty.

Now look up and read 1 John 3:10. WHOSE child are you if you don't love your brother? You are a child of the d **e v i l**!

Wow! God wants us to love others, including our enemies. Are you willing to love, pray for, bless, and feed someone who is your enemy?

____ Yes   ____ No

Matthew 5:44 HOW are you to treat your enemies? Love enemies; pray for those who persecute me.

Romans 12:14 WHAT are we do to to those who persecute us? Bless them

Romans 12:20 HOW are we to treat our enemies? Feed them if they're hungry and give them a drink if they are thirsty.

1 John 3:10 WHOSE child are you if you don't love your brother? You are a child of the d e v i l !

Discuss the rest of the text and have students answer the questions independently.

Practice saying the memory verse.

Guided Instruction

An Angry Prophet   109

If you answered no, you need to take a closer look at your heart and see if you really belong to God. Remember what it says in 1 John 3:10: The children of the devil are those who don't love their brothers.

God loves *all* people. Jesus died for people, not for plants! God doesn't want people to perish, to go to hell, to live without Him forever. That's why He sent Jesus to die for our sins—so we could be forgiven and go to heaven to live with Him!

That's also why God sent Jonah to Nineveh to warn the people of their sin and what would happen to them. He wanted them to be with Him! And it worked! The people believed God, repented (they had a change of mind), and turned from their wicked and violent ways.

Jonah didn't understand God's heart. He was also more concerned about his feelings. Jonah's thoughts were all about Jonah! WHAT about you? Are your thoughts mostly about you or others?

____

Jonah was thankful for God's compassion when God saved him from drowning and got him out of the great fish, but Jonah was not so happy when God showed compassion to the people Jonah considered his enemies (the Ninevites).

The wrong-way prophet acted the wrong way in response to God's kindness and forgiveness toward his enemies. HOW about you? Are you willing to tell kids you don't get along with that Jesus loves them and died for their sins? Is there someone you don't like very much who needs to know about Jesus? Who is it?

____

Do you think he or she needs to be told about Jesus?

_____ Yes _____ No

Remember, none of us deserves to be saved. We have all sinned

110   WEEK FIVE

and deserve to die. It's only because of God's love, compassion, and *awesome* gift of salvation that we get to go to heaven. Why don't you talk to that person and tell him or her about Jesus?

Way to go! We hope you have chosen to go the right way and not the wrong way like Jonah did. Don't forget to practice your memory verse.

(page 110)

WRITE THE STORY

"Hi, Mr. Chase!" Max called as Mr. Chase walked into the newsroom. "We can't believe that today is our last day at the *Nineveh News*. We have learned so much about being reporters and putting together a newspaper."

Molly spoke up. "Thanks so much for all your help."

"You're welcome. You guys have worked hard, and just look at all you have accomplished! You investigated the book of Jonah and discovered that Jonah is about a lot more than just a big fish. Are you ready to write your last story for the *Nineveh News?*"

Max and Molly nodded eagerly.

"Great! Then boot up those computers and tell your readers what happened after God saved Nineveh."

"Sure thing," Max replied. "Come on, Molly. Let's get started."

Okay, rookie reporter. Get started on your last assignment. Talk to God, and then turn to page 126 and read Jonah 4. WHAT is this last story about? Write an eye-catching headline

would bring upon them. And He did not do it.

(page 126)

Chapter 4

1 But it greatly displeased Jonah and he became angry.

2 He prayed to the LORD and said, "Please LORD, was not this what I said while I was still in my own country? Therefore in order to forestall this I fled to Tarshish, for I knew that You are a gracious and compassionate God, slow to anger and abundant in lovingkindness, and one who relents concerning calamity.

3 "Therefore now, O LORD, please take my life from me, for death is better to me than life."

4 The LORD said, "Do you have good reason to be angry?"

5 Then Jonah went out from the city and sat east of it. There he made a shelter for himself and sat under it in the shade until he could see what would happen in the city.

6 So the LORD God appointed a plant and it grew up over Jonah to be a shade over his head to deliver him from his discomfort. And Jonah was extremely happy about the plant.

7 But God appointed a worm when dawn came the next day and it attacked the plant and it withered.

Ask God to give you a clear mind to correctly report His story about Jonah.

Guided Instruction

117 Transfer the format of "Nineveh News, Issue 5" to large chart paper. As students read Jonah 4 fill in the chart and have them complete page 111.

NINEVEH NEWS

ISSUE 5

BREAKING NEWS!

(headline) **Jonah Gets Angry/God's Compassion**

WEATHER:

Sunny & Hot (draw a picture)

God saves Nineveh! But instead of being happy, Jonah becomes **angry** and pleads with God to take his life. God asks him, "Do you have a good reason to be angry?" Jonah leaves the city and makes a shelter. God appoints a **plant** to give Jonah shade.

Observation Worksheets—Jonah 127

8 When the sun came up God appointed a scorching east wind, and the sun beat down on Jonah's head so that he became faint and begged with all his soul to die, saying, "Death is better to me than life."

9 Then God said to Jonah, "Do you have good reason to be angry about the plant?" And he said, "I have good reason to be angry, even to death."

10 Then the LORD said, "You had compassion on the plant for which you did not work and which you did not cause to grow, which came up overnight and perished overnight.

11 "Should I not have compassion on Nineveh, the great city in which there are more than 120,000 persons who do not know the difference between their right and left hand, as well as many animals?"

(page 110)

...lk to God, and then turn to page 126 and read Jonah 4.

WHAT is this last story about? Write an eye-catching headline for the top of the newspaper.

WHAT is the weather like in Jonah 4? Draw a picture for the weather corner.

Now write your news story by filling in each of the blanks on the front page of this edition of the *Nineveh News.*

An Angry Prophet 111

117

WHAT scene in Jonah 4 do you think will get your readers' attention? Draw a front-page illustration to capture this scene.

NINEVEH NEWS

ISSUE 5

Sunny & Hot
(draw a picture)

Weather

BREAKING NEWS!

Jonah Gets Angry/God's Compassion

____
(Put your headline here)

God saves Nineveh! But instead of being happy, Jonah becomes _____**angry**_____ and pleads with
WHAT (Jonah 4:1)
God to take his life. God asks him, "Do you have a good reason to be angry?" Jonah leaves the city and makes a shelter. God appoints a _____**plant**_____ to give Jonah
WHAT (Jonah 4:6)
sh... ...Nineveh ...to God.

(page 111)

shade. The next morning God appoints a **worm** _{WHAT (Jonah 4:7)} to attack the plant. When the sun comes up, God appoints a scorching east **wind** _{WHAT (Jonah 4:8)}. And the sun beats down. Jonah is so miserable that he begs to die. God uses the plant, worm, and wind to show this wrong-way prophet that even sinful people like the Ninevites are valuable to God. God asks Jonah, "Should I not have **compassion** _{WHAT (Jonah 4:11)} on Nineveh, the great city in which there are more than 120,000 persons?"

Sources aren't sure what happened to Jonah after his conversation with God.

But Jonah's story shows us how to love people and obey God!

Fantastic! You are a great writer!

---

112   WEEK FIVE

READ ALL ABOUT IT!

You have done such an awesome job! Max and Molly thought you might like to play a fun game to test those memory skills you have developed as a *Nineveh News* top-notch reporter. You can play this game with a friend or family member. It's called *Jonah's Journey.*

Things You Need

- the game board on page 116-117
- a coin to flip
- a marker for each player (you can use candy pieces such as M&M's, buttons, or different coins)

How to Play

Flip a coin. For heads, move ahead two spaces. For tails, move ahead one space. If you land on a memory-verse square, say the verse correctly and get a free turn. If you land on a space with a number, do what the instructions with that number say.

The first player to reach Nineveh with a good attitude wins!

Guided Instruction

The next morning God appoints a **worm** to attack the plant.

When the sun comes up, God appoints a scorching east **wind**, and the sun beats down. Jonah is so miserable that he begs to die. God uses the plant, worm, and wind to show this wrong-way prophet that even sinful people like the Ninevites are valuable to God. God asks Jonah, "Should I not have **compassion** on Nineveh, the great city in which there are more than 120,000 persons?"

Jonah's story shows us how to love people and obey God!

118 Turn to page 112 and play the game *Jonah's Journey.*

Guided Instruction

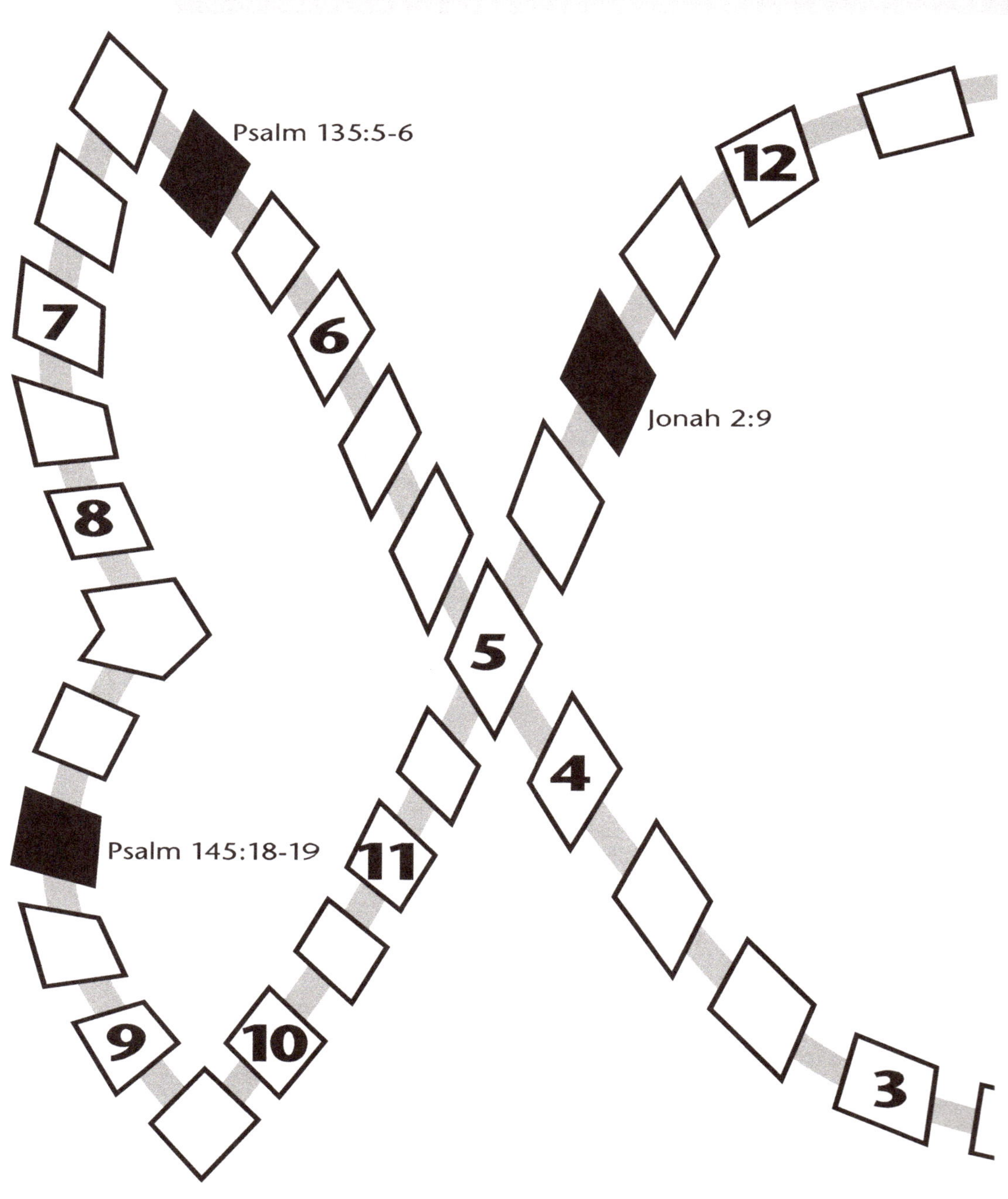

(page 117)

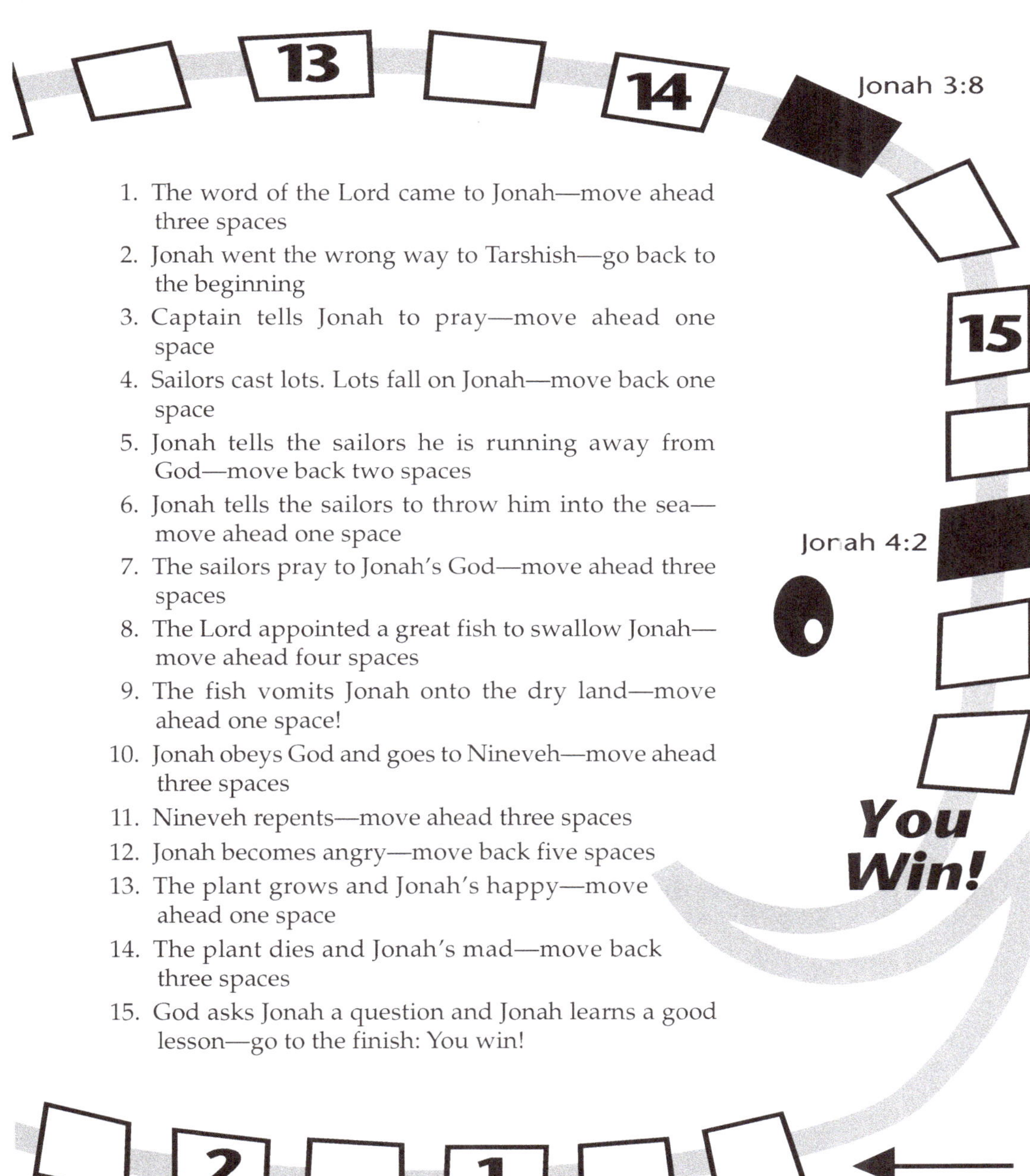

1. The word of the Lord came to Jonah—move ahead three spaces
2. Jonah went the wrong way to Tarshish—go back to the beginning
3. Captain tells Jonah to pray—move ahead one space
4. Sailors cast lots. Lots fall on Jonah—move back one space
5. Jonah tells the sailors he is running away from God—move back two spaces
6. Jonah tells the sailors to throw him into the sea—move ahead one space
7. The sailors pray to Jonah's God—move ahead three spaces
8. The Lord appointed a great fish to swallow Jonah—move ahead four spaces
9. The fish vomits Jonah onto the dry land—move ahead one space!
10. Jonah obeys God and goes to Nineveh—move ahead three spaces
11. Nineveh repents—move ahead three spaces
12. Jonah becomes angry—move back five spaces
13. The plant grows and Jonah's happy—move ahead one space
14. The plant dies and Jonah's mad—move back three spaces
15. God asks Jonah a question and Jonah learns a good lesson—go to the finish: You win!

Guided Instruction

 Read "Extra! Extra!" and finish acting out the story of Jonah. Read "Make Your Own Newspaper" on pages 112–114.

(page 112)

"EXTRA! EXTRA!"

This is your last Jonah scene to act out. God has just saved Nineveh. Show Jonah's reaction, and show how he prays to God. Get someone with a big voice to stand behind the scenes to say God's lines. Get a tall vine for your plant. Make a worm out of construction paper or you can get a Popsicle stick and glue on some craft pom-poms or material. As Jonah, be dramatic as you tell God how angry you are. Then show how loving and compassionate God is as He delivers the final lines.

What a performance!

MAKE YOUR OWN NEWSPAPER

Another fun thing you can do is create your own newspaper. Think of a name for your paper and decide what kind of stories you want to write about. Gather the facts for your stories just like you did while on assignment for the *Nineveh News.*

Interview the people who are part of your stories. Don't forget to ask the 5 W's and an H questions!

Now write your story. You can use your computer or write it by hand. Check your spelling and punctuation. Be a great editor and make any needed corrections.

Don't forget: You need some eye-catching headlines. And if you have a camera, you can take some pictures to go with your stories. If you don't have a camera, draw your pictures like you did for the *Nineveh News.*

After you have your stories just the way you want them, you are ready to make your paper. Format the page on your computer to make two columns, and then type your story into those two columns. Don't forget to leave space for your pictures!

If you don't have a computer, you can use a ruler and a pencil to draw two columns on typing paper. (See the drawing below.)

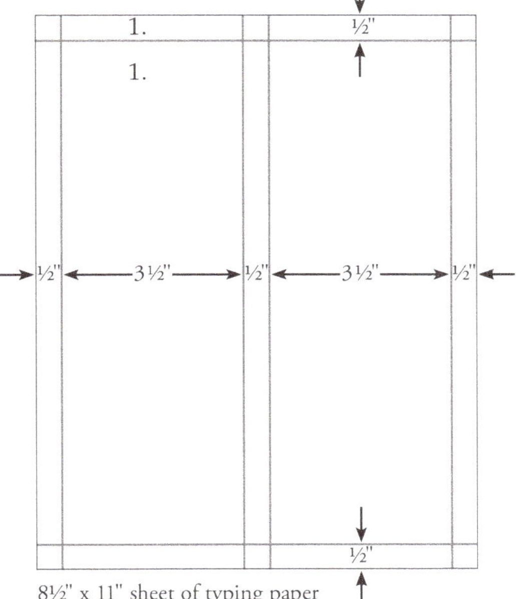

120 Make the newspaper and share it with family and friends.

Guided Instruction

121 Read and discuss "Hot Off the Press!" on page 114.

After you have your columns completed, print the name of your newspaper in large letters at the top of the paper with a bold font type on the computer or with a black marker. Arrange your pictures where you want them, and insert them on the computer or glue them on the paper. If your newspaper is more than one page, staple all the pages together. Share your newspaper with family and friends. Have fun!

HOT OFF THE PRESS!

121 You did it! Sam is about to go crazy! He is jumping up to give you a good face-licking! You have helped write the stories for the *Nineveh News* so everyone will know just how awesome God is and what He wanted Jonah to do.

Look at all you have learned. You saw that God had a plan for Jonah, and that He was faithful even when Jonah was disobedient.

You also found out that you can't run away from God; God is always with you. He knows where you are and what is in your heart.

God is sovereign. He is the ruler over everything! God hears and answers prayers! And you saw God appoint a fish, a plant, a worm, and a scorching wind to get the wrong-way prophet's attention.

And you discovered just how much God hates sin. He sent a calamity—a great storm—to stop Jonah from running away. And He was going to destroy Nineveh and all the people and animals in it. But remember, God loves you so much He will help you turn around when you are headed the wrong way!

God ended this story with a question to Jonah. God wants you to know just how important it is to be compassionate so you don't end up with a heart like Jonah's. God is compassionate and kind. He doesn't want anyone to perish. God loves you so much He gave His only Son to die on a cross so that you can live with Him forever! Why not stop and tell God thank You right now?

We are so proud of you and all your hard work! We hope that you have learned not to be a wrong-way Jonah, but to go the right way by loving and obeying God and by loving people.

Don't forget to fill out the card in the back of this book. We have something special we want to send you for spreading the news about our incredible God and a runaway prophet! We hope you'll join us for another adventure in God's Word really soon.

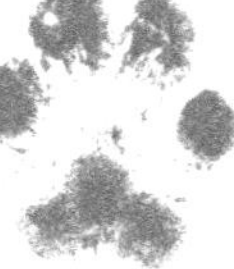

(Sam)

Guided Instruction

Use the quiz on Week Five on page 142 to check memory and understanding.

Use the Final Exam on pages 143-144 to check the kids overall understanding of *Wrong Way, Jonah.*

Play a game for the kids to review all they have learned in the book of Jonah.

You can also put on a play on the whole book for your school or church.

D4Y "Wrong Way, Jonah!" Quizzes

Week 1: Stormy Seas

1. What came to Jonah?
   a. The Word of the Lord
   b. A vision
   c. Another prophet
   d. A nightmare

2. Where did the Lord tell Jonah to go?
   a. Nineveh
   b. Joppa
   c. Tarshish
   d. Jerusalem

3. Why did God want Jonah to go to Nineveh?
   a. To see a friend
   b. To preach coming judgment on wicked-ness
   c. To pray with leaders
   d. To help the poor

4. Why did Jonah want to go to Tarshish?
   a. To meet a friend
   b. To take a vacation
   c. To flee from God
   d. To be obedient

5. What was Jonah's sin?
   a. Sleeping on board ship
   b. Fleeing from God
   c. Lying to the captain
   d. Jumping overboard

6. What did the sailors do?
   a. Cast lots
   b. Ignored Jonah
   c. Befriended Jonah
   d. Rowed out to sea

7. The sailors became ________________.
   a. Sleepy
   b. Hungry
   c. Frightened
   d. Seasick

8. What did Jonah tell the sailors to do?
   a. Protect him
   b. Pray with him
   c. Row to land
   d. Throw him overboard

9. What did the Lord do when Jonah tried to flee from Him?
   a. Hurled a great wind
   b. Helped the sailors
   c. Calmed the sea
   d. Let Jonah go where he wanted to go

10. What was the calamity?
   a. A pirate attack
   b. Overweighted cargo
   c. A great storm
   d. An undersea earthquake

Memory Verse

Psalm 135:5-6

"For I know that the Lord is great and that our Lord is above all gods. Whatever the Lord pleases, He does, in heaven and in earth, in the seas and in all deeps."

Week 2: Man Overboard

1. What did the sailors feel when Jonah told them he was fleeing from God?
   a. Indifference
   b. Fear
   c. Sadness
   d. Happiness

2. What was the condition of the sea?
   a. Stormy
   b. Calm
   c. Misty
   d. Foggy

3. Jonah told the sailor to throw him into the
   ______.
   a. Brig (hold)
   b. Galley (kitchen)
   c. Sea
   d. Banana pile

4. What did the sailors do?
   a. Rowed toward land
   b. Radioed the navy
   c. Prayed
   d. Hid in the hold

5. Then what did the men do?
   a. Took a nap
   b. Prayed to the Lord
   c. Packed to leave
   d. Sang songs

6. What did the sea do after Jonah was thrown overboard?
   a. Entered the hull
   b. Sank the ship
   c. Stopped raging
   d. Raged worse

7. The sailors offered ___________ to the Lord.
   a. Songs
   b. Sacrifice
   c. Prayers
   d. Praise

8. What did the Lord appoint to swallow Jonah?
   a. A crocodile
   b. A high wave
   c. A great fish
   d. A great flush

9. Where was Jonah then?
   a. In the fish's stomach
   b. In the wave
   c. On the ocean floor
   d. On the ship

10. How long was Jonah there?
    a. A week
    b. A day and a night
    c. Three days and three nights
    d. A month

Memory Verse

Psalm 145:18–19

"The Lord is near to a l who call upon Him, to all who call upon Him in truth. He will fulfill the desire of those who fear Him; He will also hear their cry and will save them."

Week 3: Inside the Great Fish

1. What did Jonah do in the fish's stomach?
   - a. Prayed to the Lord
   - b. Sat down
   - c. Tried to get out
   - d. Slept

2. How did Jonah feel in the fish?
   - a. Sleepy
   - b. Distressed
   - c. Curious
   - d. Hungry

3. God heard Jonah's _____________.
   - a. Voice
   - b. Song
   - c. Story
   - d. Laugh

4. God had the fish __________Jonah up on dry land.
   - a. Shake
   - b. Carry
   - c. Vomit
   - d. Throw

5. What was wrapped around Jonah's head?
   - a. Weeds
   - b. Fish
   - c. Eels
   - d. Scarf

6. What did Jonah remember to do?
   - a. Sing hymns
   - b. Pray to God
   - c. Sleep
   - d. Eat

7. What did Jonah say he will do?
   - a. Sacrifice to God
   - b. Sleep
   - c. Hide
   - d. Eat

8. What did Jonah *specifically* realize is from the Lord?
   - a. Fish
   - b. Punishment
   - c. Salvation
   - d. A good time

9. Where did God tell Jonah to go?
   - a. Jerusalem
   - b. Nineveh
   - c. Joppa
   - d. Tarshish

10. Where did Jonah try to go instead?
   - a. Jerusalem
   - b. Nineveh
   - c. Joppa
   - d. Tarshish

Memory Verse

Jonah 2:9

"But I will sacrifice to you, with the voice of thanksgiving. That which I have vowed I will pay. Salvation is from the Lord."

Week 4: A Second Chance

1. What was the source of Jonah's knowledge of what to do?
   a. God
   b. Himself (a dream)
   c. An angel
   d. Another prophet

2. Where did Jonah *finally* go?
   a. Joppa
   b. Tarshish
   c. Nineveh
   d. Jerusalem

3. This city is in _______________.
   a. Israel
   b. Africa
   c. Iran
   d. Assyria

4. What did God say Nineveh is full of?
   a. Wickedness
   b. Poverty
   c. Mercy
   d. Compassion

5. God said Nineveh will be _______________ in 40 days.
   a. Attacked
   b. Overthrown
   c. Celebrated
   d. Blessed

6. What does God tell Jonah to do?
   a. Proclaim a warning
   b. Speak to a king
   c. Pray for the people
   d. Make friends

7. How did the people respond to Jonah's message?
   a. Believed God and repented
   b. Did not believe God and stayed the same
   c. Ignored God
   d. Cursed God

8. What did the people do?
   a. Partied
   b. Sang songs
   c. Called a fast and put on sackcloth
   d. Called a feast

9. Who covered himself with sackcloth and sat on ashes?
   a. The people
   b. The king
   c. The children
   d. The ladies

10. What does the king want God to do?
    a. Withdraw His anger
    b. Punish his people
    c. Ignore his people
    d. Carry out His anger

Memory Verse

Jonah 3:8

"Let men call on God earnestly that each may turn from his wicked way and from the violence which is in his hands."

Week 5: An Angry Prophet

1. When God relented of his anger, how did Jonah feel?
    a. Happy
    b. Impatient
    c. Angry
    d. Sleepy

2. Jonah already knew that God was a ________________God.
    a. Sad
    b. Compassionate
    c. Impatient
    d. Disgusted

3. What does Jonah tell God to take?
    a. His life
    b. His clothes
    c. The Ninevites' lives
    d. A nap

4. Jonah was sheltered in the shade of a __________.
    a. Building
    b. Plant
    c. Tent
    d. Fort

5. Jonah had a bad __________about God's relenting anger.
    a. Guess
    b. Memory
    c. Attitude
    d. Dream

6. What did God appoint to kill the plant?
    a. Snow
    b. Storm
    c. Drought
    d. Worm

7. What did God send next?
    a. Scorching wind
    b. Storm
    c. Earthquake
    d. Flood

8. What does God want the people to do?
    a. Pray
    b. Wear sackcloth
    c. Repent
    d. Feast

9. What does God want this for?
    a. Their physical health
    b. Their salvation from judgment
    c. Their popularity
    d. Their hunger

10. What did God do for the world?
    a. Sent His Son
    b. Sent the devil
    c. Sent teachers
    d. Composed hymns

Memory Verse

Jonah 4:2

"You are a gracious and compassionate God, slow to anger and abundant in lovingkindness, and one who relents concerning calamity."

D4Y "Wrong Way, Jonah!" Final Exam

1. Where did the Lord tell Jonah to go?
   a. Nineveh
   b. Joppa
   c. Tarshish
   d. Jerusalem

2. Why did God want Jonah to go to Nineveh?
   a. To see a friend
   b. To preach coming judgment on wickedness
   c. To pray for leaders
   d. To help the poor

3. What was Jonah's *sin?*
   a. Sleeping on board ship
   b. Lying to the captain
   c. Fleeing from God
   d. Jumping overboard

4. What did the Lord do when Jonah tried to flee from Him?
   a. Hurled a great wind
   b. Helped the sailors
   c. Calmed the sea
   d. Let Jonah go where he wanted to go

5. What was the calamity?
   a. A pirate attack
   b. Overweighted cargo
   c. An undersea earthquake
   d. A great storm

6. What was the *primary* weather condition?
   a. Foggy
   b. Stormy
   c. Misty
   d. Calm

7. Jonah told the sailors to throw him into the __________.
   a. Brig (hold)
   b. Galley (kitchen)
   c. Sea
   d. Banana pile

8. What did the sailors do?
   a. Rowed toward land
   b. Radioed the navy
   c. Prayed
   d. Hid in the hold

9. What did the sea do after Jonah was thrown overboard?
   a. Entered the hull
   b. Sank the ship
   c. Stopped raging
   d. Raged worse

10. What did the Lord appoint to swallow Jonah?
    a. A crocodile
    b. A great fish
    c. A high wave
    d. A great flush

11. How did Jonah feel in the fish?
    a. Sleepy
    b. Curious
    c. Distressed
    d. Hungry

12. How long did God leave Jonah in the fish's stomach?
    a. A month
    b. Three days and nights
    c. A day
    d. A week

13. God had the fish __________ Jonah up on dry land.
    a. Shake
    b. Vomit
    c. Throw
    d. Carry

14. What did Jonah remember to do?
    a. Sing hymns
    b. Pray to God
    c. Sleep
    d. Eat

15. What did Jonah *specifically* realize is from the Lord?
    a. Fish
    b. Punishment
    c. Salvation
    d. A good time

16. What did God say Nineveh is full of?
    a. Wickedness
    b. Charity
    c. Love
    d. Mercy

17. What does God tell Jonah to do?
    a. Proclaim a warning to all
    b. Speak to a king
    c. Pray for the people
    d. Make friends

18. How did the people respond to Jonah's message?
    a. Cursed God
    b. Believed God and repented
    c. Did not believe God and stayed the same
    d. Ignored God

19. What does the king want God to do?
    a. Punish his people
    b. Ignore his people
    c. Withdraw His anger
    d. Carry out His anger

20. When God relented of His anger, how did Jonah feel?
    a. Happy
    b. Angry
    c. Sleepy
    d. Impatient

21. What does Jonah tell God to take?
    a. His life
    b. His clothes
    c. The Ninevites' lives
    d. A nap

22. Jonah had a bad _________ about God's relenting anger.
    a. Guess
    b. Memory
    c. Attitude
    d. Dream

23. What does God want the people to do?
    a. Pray
    b. Repent
    c. Wear sackcloth
    d. Feast

24. What does God want the people to do this (previous question) *for?*
    a. Their salvation from judgment
    b. Their physical health
    c. Their popularity
    d. Their hunger

25. What did God do for the world?
    a. Sent the devil
    b. Sent His Son
    c. Sent teachers
    d. Composed hymns

Quiz Answer Key

Week 1	Week 2	Week 3	Week 4	Week 5
1. a	1. b	1. a	1. a	1. c
2. a	2. a	2. b	2. c	2. b
3. b	3. c	3. a	3. d	3. a
4. c	4. a	4. c	4. a	4. b
5. b	5. b	5. a	5. b	5. c
6. a	6. c	6. b	6. a	6. d
7. c	7. b	7. a	7. a	7. a
8. d	8. c	8. c	8. c	8. c
9. a	9. a	9. b	9. b	9. b
10. c	10. c	10. d	10. a	10. a

Final Answer Key

1. a	14. b
2. b	15. c
3. c	16. a
4. a	17. a
5. d	18. b
6. b	19. c
7. c	20. b
8. a	21. a
9. c	22. c
10. b	23. b
11. c	24. a
12. b	25. b
13. b	

Optional Games

Drawing Game

To play the drawing game you will need to type out what you want the kids to draw such as the people and events in Jonah on a piece of paper and cut them out individually.

Fold each slip of paper and place it in a zip-loc bag or a bowl.

Divide your class into two teams.

Have a child from Team 1 come up to the front of the class and draw out a slip of paper out of the bag. After he or she has picked a slip of paper he or she will draw a sketch to depict what they have chosen on the whiteboard. Both teams watch as the child draws their sketch. When a child from either team thinks they know what is being drawn they may raise their hand and you call on the child whose hand you see first. It can be a child from either team. If the answer is not guessed continue letting them guess until someone guesses the correct answer.

When the answer is guessed correctly, the team who answered the question receives 100 points for their team. Then, the teacher asks the student who guessed the drawing correctly a question that goes with that drawing. For example, if they were drawing "the Word of the Lord comes to Jonah", the teacher might ask, "WHO is Jonah, WHAT did we learn about him?" If the student answers the question correctly they receive another 100 points for their team for a total of 200 points. If they answer incorrectly, someone from the other team gets a chance to answer the question and receive 100 points for their team, with each team receiving 100 points.

After the points are given, it's Team 2's turn to pick a slip of paper out of the bag and draw the next beast, person, or event. Go back and forth with each team until each paper is picked and drawn on the whiteboard. You may want to reward the winning team with a treat like a small piece of candy or a privilege.

Optional Games

The Matching Game

You need at least ten questions and answers from the lesson you are studying.

Type the answers on a sheet of paper. Make two sets of answers and cut the answers into individual strips and place each set of answers in an envelope.

Divide your class into two teams. Pick a student from each team and have them come up and stand in front of you, opposite each other (back to back) in the middle of the room. On each side of the room you have taken the answers out of each envelope and mixed them up and placed them in two piles on the floor.

You ask a question and tap the two students in front of you and say "Go." They have to run from you to their side of the room and look for the correct answer to the question you just asked in their pile. If they bring you an incorrect answer, tell them, "Wrong, try again" and they race back again to find the correct answer. The first one to race back to you and bring you the correct answer gets 100 points for their team. You continue to do this until you have answered all your questions and the team with the most points wins.

Optional Games

M&M® Draw

If you are working with one student you can still play the game by asking the questions and letting the child answer and draw an M&M® if he/she answers correctly. Tell them if they get to a certain number of points they will receive a reward or privilege.

You will need a bag of M&Ms®. Empty them into a container you can't see through. Write the point values for the M&Ms® on a white board for all the kids to see. I choose point values depending on how many there are of each color—the more there are of a color the lower the point value.

Brown: 100 points

Red: 200 points

Yellow: 300 points

Green: 400 points

Blue: 500 points

Orange: 600 points

Divide the kids into two teams and ask a question from the lesson or book you are studying. If the kid you pick from the first team answers the question correctly, he or she closes their eyes and picks an M&M® from the container. Once they have chosen a color, they get to eat the candy and you record the points they won on the board for their team. If they miss the question, the other team gets to steal the question and draw the M&M®; then it's that team's turn to answer a question. The team with the most points wins.

Reward them with a small piece of candy or a privilege.

Learn how

you can be involved in "Establishing People in God's Word" at **precept.org/connect**

 Precept.org/connect

Use your smartphone to get connected
to Precept's ministry initiatives!
Precept.org/connect

Precept Online Community

provides support, training opportunities, and exclusive resources to help
Bible study leaders and students.

 Precept.org/POC

Use your smartphone to connect to Precept
Online Community! **Precept.org/POC**

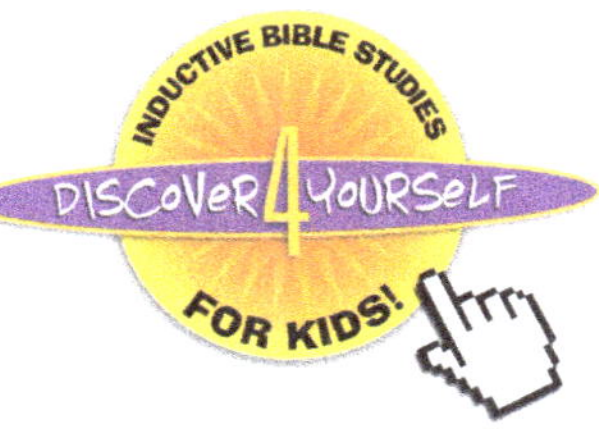

Join The Discover 4 Yourself Inductive Bible Studies for Kids! Group in Precept Online Community